Praise for *The Cloud Data Lake*

Rukmani gives the business and technical community a thoughtful and unbiased tour of modern data and analytics technologies. She uncovers first principles, empowering decision makers to understand if building a data lake makes sense for them.

—*Gordon Wong, Founder, Wong Decisions*

Highly recommended reading for cloud solution architects for understanding the emerging cloud data lake architectures.

—*Chidamber Kulkarni, Cloud Solutions Architect at Intel*

We are in the cloud era with almost unlimited cheap storage and lots of processing power, a time when companies want to migrate to the cloud. To have a successful story, those who make decisions need to understand what a data lake is; why, when, and where it is needed; what aspects can be tuned together; and their pros and cons. This book is the answer to this need.

It is helpful that the book details the available table formats, cloud offerings, and frameworks that can be used to process data, the storage layer, and then how to put these together for a performant solution suited for your needs. The decision framework that Rukmani provides in the book will help you make an informed decision on which kind of data lake to choose.

This book is a must read for every person in the big data field.

—*Andrei Ionescu, Senior Software Engineer, Adobe*

With data analytics workloads migrating to the cloud, getting an understanding of end-to-end architecture provides the necessary context to make the right trade-offs to build and support required data infrastructure tailored to various use-cases. *The Cloud Data Lake* provided me with the essential understanding needed to support data workloads in the cloud.

—*Prasanna Sundararajan, Principal Software Architect,*
Microsoft Azure

The Cloud Data Lake

A Guide to Building Robust
Cloud Data Architecture

Rukmani Gopalan

Beijing · Boston · Farnham · Sebastopol · Tokyo

The Cloud Data Lake

by Rukmani Gopalan

Published by O'Reilly Media, Inc., 1005 Gravenstein Highway North, Sebastopol, CA 95472.

O'Reilly books may be purchased for educational, business, or sales promotional use. Online editions are also available for most titles (*http://oreilly.com*). For more information, contact our corporate/institutional sales department: 800-998-9938 or *corporate@oreilly.com*.

Acquisitions Editor: Andy Kwan	**Indexer:** Sue Klefstad
Development Editor: Jill Leonard	**Interior Designer:** David Futato
Production Editor: Ashley Stussy	**Cover Designer:** Karen Montgomery
Copyeditor: Shannon Turlington	**Illustrator:** Kate Dullea
Proofreader: Piper Editorial Consulting, LLC	

December 2022:   First Edition

Revision History for the First Edition
2022-12-09:   First Release

See *http://oreilly.com/catalog/errata.csp?isbn=9781098116583* for release details.

978-1-098-11658-3

[LSI]

Table of Contents

Preface

Its six in the morning; your phone gently wakes you up and automatically turns on your notifications. Your smart refrigerator reminds you that you need to order milk and shows you an option to place an order to buy more since it knows you are running low. You do that and hop on your exercise machine, where you see personalized picks based on your workout routines. You get ready and eat breakfast without bothering to look at the clock because you know your phone will tell you when it is time to start driving based on what it has learned about your commute and the traffic patterns. As you leave, your smart home assistant ensures the lights are turned off and the doors are locked. What would have seemed like science fiction a few decades ago is a regular day in our lives now. All this is possible because of the leaps technology has made in three key areas: devices that have made computing ubiquitous, connectivity that has shrunk the world by bringing the knowledge of the internet to these devices, and technology (data, artificial intelligence, machine learning) that has helped devices learn patterns and make decisions. Data is now at the heart of how the world operates, and organizations increasingly rely on data to both inform and transform their businesses.

My mind goes back to 2013, when my own personal journey with data started as I worked on identity and personalization services for Microsoft Office. It was a year of a great many learnings for me. I understood what it meant to develop cloud-based applications, including the nuances of building a direct-to-consumer experience versus an enterprise-ready application. Most of all, though, I was thrilled at the possibility of having a direct connection to customer experiences from these cloud services. When we shipped boxed products (i.e., products that shipped in a CD or DVD) and had customers install them on their devices, the only way for us to understand their experiences was to get anonymized telemetry data, to organize user research studies or focus groups, or reading through support cases when the customer had issues. Many of our insights on product usage were based on data from the customers who opted to talk to us, which was a minute fraction. With the cloud services I built, I had a real-time understanding of my customers. This helped us tune our services and deliver more personalized experiences to our users. We were able to experiment with variations of features with our customers to better understand what helps more with their productivity. Since then, I have been working on various platforms and cloud services, and I realize how the value of the data, when amplified by the elasticity of the cloud, can help inform and transform businesses.

Why I Wrote This Book

I have engaged with hundreds of customers over the years across various industries—health care, consumer goods, retail, and manufacturing, to name a few—and I have helped them with their big data analytics needs on the cloud. I have also driven the migration of my organization's on-premises analytics workload to the cloud for better cost management as well as to take advantage of emerging technologies in machine learning. Understandably so, each of these customers comes to me with different motivations and problems. However, one common thread binds them all: the strong desire to get value out of their data. The same customers who I was talking to about the fundamentals of big data analytics five years ago have now progressed to operating very mature implementations and running more of their business-critical workloads on the data lake. As part of these conversations, there have been a few key questions that boil down to setting up, organizing, securing, and optimizing data lake implementations. In the ideal scenario, these considerations are baked into the data lake architecture design, and in some unfortunate instances, we talk about these issues when customers have a problem forcing a rearchitecture or redesign.

The promise of the infinite possibilities of leveraging a cloud data lake comes with the flip side of understanding and handling the complexities involved in building and operationalizing a cloud data lake application. I believe that while the industry works on simplifying this process over time, a foundational understanding of the concepts of a cloud data lake solution goes a long way toward building robust data lake architectures that stand the test of time. I have thoroughly enjoyed helping my customers, partners, and teams build this foundational understanding and watching them become completely empowered to drive transformational insights for their teams or organizations.

In this book, I hope to condense all these conversations and the associated lessons learned to provide an approach for data practitioners that will help you design a scalable cloud data lake architecture that informs and transforms your business.

Who Should Read This Book?

This book is primarily targeted at data architects, data developers, and data ops professionals who want to get a broad understanding of the various aspects of setting up and operating their cloud data lake. At the end of this book, you will have an understanding of the following:

- The benefits of a cloud-based big data strategy for your organization
- Architecture and design choices, including the modern data warehouse, data lakehouse, and data mesh
- Guidance and best practices for designing performant and scalable data lakes
- Data governance principles, strategies, and design choices

Whether you are taking your first steps or looking at modernizing your data lake on the cloud, my hope is that you will be prepared to have an informed, educated design conversation with your cloud provider and your engineering teams, and you will be able to plan and budget for your engineering investments in terms of time, effort, and money. Big data analytics is one of the areas where development, technologies, and paradigm shifts happen in the blink of an eye. To me, this illustrates the abundant opportunities that are now possible. I will keep the considerations neutral of any specific technology, so when a new technology emerges, we will be able to apply these fundamentals in the context of all the available technology choices.

Introducing Klodars Corporation

In this book, we will apply the concepts of the cloud data lake to a fictitious organization, Klodars Corporation, to best illustrate them using a business problem that will resonate with most of us.

Klodars Corporation is a fictitious organization that sells umbrellas and rain gear in Seattle, Washington (cliche much?). In addition to website sales, Klodars employs salespeople to reach out to retailers to sell its umbrellas as a bulk distribution in the Seattle area. It has a small software development team that writes applications to manage inventory and sales, leveraging SQL server as the operational database running on servers that are maintained in its offices. It also leverages Salesforce to manage its customer profiles and interactions.

Because of the quality of its rain gear and excellent sales channels, Klodars Corporation is rapidly expanding across the state of Washington as well as in the neighboring states of Oregon and Idaho. Its direct-to-consumer business is taking off through its website, and its marketing department is running excellent campaigns on social media. In addition, Klodars wants to expand its business to sell winter gear based on customer demand. So it plans to acquire another business that sells winter gear. While this is amazing news for the business, it is at that inflection point where its database technology doesn't quite scale to its increasing needs, and it is evaluating a move to the cloud.

Navigating the Book

While I recommend that you read this book end to end for a complete understanding, each chapter is self-contained, and you can focus on specific topics depending on what is top of your mind. You can also come back to this book at any point to reference specific sections without having to read from the beginning.

- At the end of Chapter 1, you will get an overall understanding of what *cloud data lake* means and its benefits. You will also understand that moving to the cloud involves thinking through design considerations and making an informed choice, as opposed to going with a lift-and-shift approach.

- In Chapter 2, I will go over the various cloud data lake architectures, and you will understand the value proposition of each architecture. At the end of this chapter, you will be able to build on the foundational understanding of Chapter 1 and know about the scenarios that these cloud architectures solve as well as get concrete examples of how an organization can leverage these architectures.

- Data is the new gold, oil, bacon…insert your favorite metaphor here. The key to a cloud data lake architecture is a robust design of your data layer, which lays the foundation of every scenario you build on it. Chapter 3 will get into the details of the foundational layer of your data lake and the various aspects of designing, organizing, and managing your data in the data lake. I strongly advise that you give this chapter a lot of attention to help you design your data lake not only to meet your immediate needs but also to scale as your business grows.

- In Chapter 4, I will talk about the various considerations for designing your data lake for scale. I will also provide a set of best practices for you to consider as you are building your data estate and data pipelines. Chapters 5 and 6 will deep dive into two aspects: tuning your cloud data lake to meet the desired performance and data formats that serve as critical building blocks for performance.

- In Chapter 7, based on the learnings from the chapters before, I will introduce a decision framework that you can use to make the right choices for your data lake architecture. I will also provide a checklist you can use for an easy reference.

- Chapter 8 is a catchall section for questions that may not have been answered earlier in the book. As I mentioned before, the data lake community is growing and rapidly innovating as we learn more every day. You have an opportunity to influence these innovations and bring your own ideas to the table. In the meantime, let us focus on progress, not perfection; there is ample value that comes out of just this progression.

In summary, after reading this book, you will understand the fundamentals of everything it takes to build a cloud data lake and will be able to apply this understanding in many ways, including the following:

- Use the design choices in the book to build out a data strategy that scales as the organizational and business needs grow
- Pitch to key decision makers how a lean data platform team can drive key business transformations using a robust data strategy
- Empower your organization to focus on the key business problems with a scalable data infrastructure
- Realize more value from data using advanced analytics offerings on the cloud

Conventions Used in This Book

The following typographical conventions are used in this book:

Italic
:   Indicates new terms, URLs, email addresses, filenames, and file extensions.

`Constant width`
:   Used for program listings, as well as within paragraphs to refer to program elements such as variable or function names, databases, data types, environment variables, statements, and keywords.

`Constant width bold`
:   Shows commands or other text that should be typed literally by the user.

`Constant width italic`
:   Shows text that should be replaced with user-supplied values or by values determined by context.

> This element signifies a tip or suggestion.

> This element signifies a general note.

This element indicates a warning or caution.

O'Reilly Online Learning

 For more than 40 years, *O'Reilly Media* has provided technology and business training, knowledge, and insight to help companies succeed.

Our unique network of experts and innovators share their knowledge and expertise through books, articles, and our online learning platform. O'Reilly's online learning platform gives you on-demand access to live training courses, in-depth learning paths, interactive coding environments, and a vast collection of text and video from O'Reilly and 200+ other publishers. For more information, visit *http://oreilly.com*.

How to Contact Us

Please address comments and questions concerning this book to the publisher:

> O'Reilly Media, Inc.
> 1005 Gravenstein Highway North
> Sebastopol, CA 95472
> 800-998-9938 (in the United States or Canada)
> 707-829-0515 (international or local)
> 707-829-0104 (fax)

We have a web page for this book, where we list errata, examples, and any additional information. You can access this page at *https://oreil.ly/the-cloud-data-lake-1e*.

Email *bookquestions@oreilly.com* to comment or ask technical questions about this book.

For news and information about our books and courses, visit *https://oreilly.com*.

Find us on LinkedIn: *https://linkedin.com/company/oreilly-media*

Follow us on Twitter: *https://twitter.com/oreillymedia*

Watch us on YouTube: *https://www.youtube.com/oreillymedia*

Acknowledgments

As the proverbial idiom goes, it takes a village to write a book, and I'm eternally grateful to the multitude of folks who helped in making this book a reality.

First and foremost, I would like to deeply thank my teams, customers, and partners at Microsoft during my tenure with Microsoft Office, Azure HDInsight, and Azure Data Lake Storage/Cosmos for building my understanding of the data space and trusting my instincts and approach as I impacted the transformational insights of various organizations with these offerings. The list of people here is so long that I could fill a book with all their names.

Thanks to Tomer Shiran from Dremio and the team at Monte Carlo—Barr Moses, Lior Gavish, and Molly Vorwerck—for your enlightening interviews on data lakehouse and data observability that turned into great sidebars for the book.

The team at O'Reilly has been amazing at helping me shape my thoughts and approach into this book. Jill Leonard and Andy Kwan—thanks for being there every step of the way, whether it was discussing the structuring of certain topics and the appropriate level of details or, many times, helping me with my multiple bouts of impostor syndrome.

A huge shoutout to the tech reviewers who took the time to read through the book and shared their very valuable insights and feedback: Shreya Pal, Andrei Ionescu, Alicia Moniz, Prasanna Sundararajan, Chidamber Kulkarni, Gordon Wong, Gareth Eager, Vinoth Chandar, and Vini Jaiswal. You really helped me understand a reader's journey, which offered valuable lessons for life.

Finally, no words will ever express the gratitude I feel toward my family—my awesome husband, Sriram Govindarajan, and my amazing kids, Anish Bharadwaj and Dhanya Bharadwaj, for being the constant source of inspiration and support for me, not just for this book but for life. Thanks to Janaki Gopalan and Gopalan Krishnamachari, my mom and dad, who are not with me anymore physically but stay with me forever in the core values they have instilled in me around hard work, accountability, and unconditional giving.

CHAPTER 1

Big Data—Beyond the Buzz

Without big data, you are blind and deaf and in the middle of a freeway.
—Geoffrey Moore

If we were playing workplace bingo, there is a big chance you would win by crossing off all these terms that you have heard in your organization in the past three months: digital transformation, data strategy, transformational insights, data lake, warehouse, data science, machine learning, and intelligence. It is now common knowledge that data is a key ingredient for organizations to succeed, and organizations that rely on data and AI clearly outperform their contenders. According to an IDC study sponsored by Seagate (*https://oreil.ly/J8fjX*), the amount of data that is captured, collected, or replicated is expected to grow to *175 zettabytes (ZB)* by the year 2025. This data that is captured, collected, or replicated is referred to as the *Global DataSphere*. This data comes from three classes of sources:

The core
Traditional or cloud-based datacenters

The edge
Hardened infrastructure, such as cell towers

The endpoints
PCs, tablets, smartphones, and Internet of Things (IoT) devices

This study also predicts that *49% of this Global DataSphere* will be residing in public cloud environments by the year 2025.

If you have ever wondered, "Why does this data need to be stored? What is it good for?" the answer is very simple. Think of all of this data as pieces of words strewn around the globe in different languages, each sharing a sliver of information, like pieces of a puzzle. Stitching them together in a meaningful fashion tells a story that not only informs but also could transform businesses, people, and even the way the world runs. Most successful organizations already leverage data to understand the growth drivers for their businesses and perceived customer experiences and to take the rightful action; looking at "the funnel," or customer acquisition, adoption, engagement, and retention, is now largely the lingua franca of funding product investments. These types of data processing and analysis are referred to as *business intelligence*, or BI, and classified as "offline insights." Essentially, the data and the insights are crucial in presenting the trend that shows growth so business leaders can take action; however, this workstream is separate from the core business logic used to run the business itself. As the maturity of the data platform grows, an inevitable signal we get from all customers is that they start getting more requests to run more scenarios on their data lakes, truly adhering to the idiom "Data is the new oil."

Organizations leverage data to understand the growth drivers for their businesses and perceived customer experience. They can then use data to set targets and drive improvements in customer experience with better support and newer features. They can also create better marketing strategies to grow their businesses and drive efficiencies to lower their costs of building their products and organizations. Starbucks, the coffee shop that is present around the globe, uses data in every place possible to continuously measure and improve its business. As explained in this YouTube video (*https://oreil.ly/Rnkz6*), Starbucks uses the data from its mobile applications and correlates the data with its ordering system to better understand customer usage patterns and send targeted marketing campaigns. It uses sensors on its coffee machines that emit health data every few seconds, and this data is analyzed to drive improvements into its predictive maintenance. It also uses these connected coffee machines to download recipes to them without involving human intervention.

As the world is just learning to cope with the COVID-19 pandemic, organizations are leveraging data heavily not only to transform their businesses but also to measure the health and productivity of their organizations to help their employees feel connected and minimize burnout. Overall, data is also used for world-saving initiatives such as Project Zamba (*https://oreil.ly/emc3D*), which uses AI for wildlife research and conservation in the remote jungles of Africa, as well as leverages IoT and data science to create a circular economy to promote environmental sustainability.

What Is Big Data?

All of the examples given previously share a few things in common:

- These scenarios illustrate that data can be explored and consumed in a variety of ways, and when the data is generated, there is not really a clear idea of the consumption patterns. This is different from traditional online transaction processing (OLTP) and online analytical processing (OLAP) systems, where the data is specifically designed and curated to solve specific business problems.

- Data can come in all kinds of shapes and formats: it can be a few bytes emitted from an IoT sensor, social media data dumps, files from line of business (LOB) systems and relational databases, and sometimes even audio and video content.

- The processing scenarios of big data are vastly different—whether they are data science, SQL-like queries, or any other custom processing.

- As studies show, big data is not just high volume but can also arrive at various speeds: as one large dump, such as data ingested in batches from relational databases, or continuously streamed, like clickstream or IoT data.

These are some of the characteristics of big data. *Big data processing* refers to the set of tools and technologies used to store, manage, and analyze data without posing any restrictions or assumptions on the source, format, or size of the data.

The goal of big data processing is to analyze a large amount of data with varying quality and generate high-value insights. The sources of data that we saw previously, whether IoT sensors or social media dumps, have signals in them that are valuable to the business. As an example, social media feeds have indicators of customer sentiments: whether they loved a product and tweeted about it or had issues that they complained about. These signals are hidden amid a large volume of other data, creating a lower value density—you need to scrub a large amount of data to get a small amount of signal. In some cases, chances are that you might not have any signals at all. Needle in a haystack much?

Further, a signal by itself might not tell you much; however, when you combine two weak signals, you get a stronger signal. As an example, sensor data from vehicles tells you how often brakes are used or accelerators are pressed, traffic data gives patterns of traffic, and car sales data provides information on who got what cars. Although these data sources are disparate, insurance companies could correlate the vehicle sensor data and traffic patterns to build a profile of how safe the driver is, thereby offering lower insurance rates to drivers with safe driving profiles.

As seen in Figure 1-1, a big data processing system enables the correlation of a large amount of data with varied value density (value density can be considered as signal-to-noise ratio) to generate insights with definite high-value density. These insights have the power to drive critical transformations to products, processes, and organizational cultures.

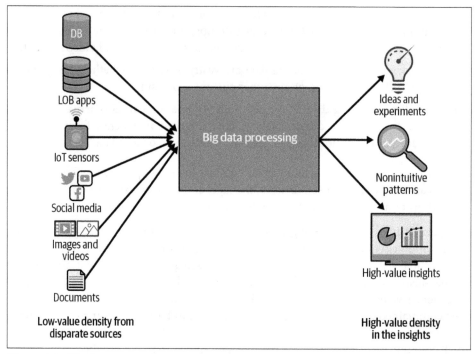

Figure 1-1. Big data processing overview

Big data is typically characterized by six Vs. Fun fact—a few years ago, we characterized big data with only three Vs: *v*olume, *v*elocity, and *v*ariety. We have already added
three more Vs: *v*alue, *v*eracity, and *v*ariability. This only goes to show how more
dimensions were unearthed in just a few years. Well, who knows, by the time this
book is published, maybe more Vs will be added! Let's now take a look at the Vs:

Volume

This is the "big" part of big data, referring to the size of the datasets being processed. When databases or data warehouses refer to *hyperscale*, that could mean
tens or hundreds of terabytes (TB), and, in rare instances, petabytes (PB), of data.
In addition, you could have thousands of columns in your datasets contributing
to another dimension of volume. In the world of big data processing, PBs of data
is more the norm, and larger data lakes easily grow to hundreds of PBs as more
and more scenarios run on the data lake. Something to note here is that volume
is a spectrum in big data. You need to have a system that works well for TBs of
data and that can scale just as well as these TBs accumulate to hundreds of PBs.
This enables your organization to start small and scale as your business as well as
your data estate grow.

Velocity

Data in the big data ecosystem has different "speeds" associated with it, in terms of how quickly it is generated and how fast it moves and changes. For example, think of trends in social media. While a video on TikTok could go viral, a few days later, it is completely irrelevant, leaving room for the next trend. In the same vein, think of health care data such as your daily steps; while it is critical information for measuring your activity at the time, it's less of a signal a few days later. In these examples, you have millions, sometimes even billions, of events generated at scale that need to be ingested, and insights generated in near real time, whether that is real-time recommendations of what hashtags are trending or how far away you are from your daily goal. On the other hand, you have scenarios where the value of data persists over a long time. For example, sales forecasting and budget planning heavily relies on trends over past years and leverages data that has persisted over the past few months or years. A big data system to support both of these scenarios—ingesting a large amount of data in batches as well as continuously streaming data and being able to process it—lets you have the flexibility of running a variety of scenarios on your data lake and correlate data from these various sources to generate insights that would have not been possible before. For example, you could predict sales based on long-term patterns as well as quick trends from social media using the same system.

Variety

As we saw in the first Vs, big data processing systems accommodate a spectrum of scenarios. Key to that is supporting a variety of data. Big data processing systems have the ability to process data without imposing any restrictions on the size, structure, or source of the data. They provide the ability for you to work on structured data (database tables, LOB systems) that have a defined tabular structure and strong guarantees, semistructured data (data in flexibly defined structures, such as CSVs and JSON), and unstructured data (images, social media feeds, video, text files, etc.). This allows you to get signals from sources that are valuable (think insurance or mortgage documents) without making any assumptions on what the data format is.

Most data warehouses promise the ability to scale to multiple PBs of data and operate on unstructured data, and they are relentlessly improving support for both higher volume and variety. It's important to remember that data warehouses are not designed to store and process tens or hundreds of PBs, at least as they stand today. An additional consideration is cost, where, depending on your scenarios, it could be a lot cheaper to store data in your data lake as compared with the data warehouse. Additionally, while data warehouses offer support for unstructured data, their highly optimized path is to process structured data that is in a proprietary format specific to that warehouse. Although the line between data lakes and data warehouses continues to blur, it is important to keep these original value propositions in mind when picking the right architecture for your data platform.

Veracity

Veracity refers to the quality and origin of big data. A big data analytics system accepts data without any assumptions on the format or the source, which means that naturally not all data is powered with highly structured insights. For example, your smart fridge could send a few bytes of information indicating its device health status, and some of this information could be lost or imperfect depending on the implementation. Big data processing systems need to incorporate a data preparation phase, when data is examined, cleansed, and curated before complex operations are performed.

Variability

Whether it is the size, the structure, the source, or the quality, variability is the name of the game in big data systems. Any processing system for big data needs to incorporate variability to be able to operate on any and all types of data. In addition, the processing systems can define the structure of the data they want on demand—this is referred to as applying a schema on demand. As an example, if you have taxi data that has a CSV of hundreds of data points, one processing system could focus on the values corresponding to source and destination while ignoring the rest, and another could focus on driver identification and pricing while ignoring the rest. This is the biggest power: every system by itself contains a piece of the puzzle, and getting them all together reveals insights like never before. I once worked with a financial services company that collected data from various counties on housing and land; they got data as Microsoft Excel files, CSV dumps, or highly structured database backups. They processed this data and aggregated it to generate excellent insights into land values, house values, and buying patterns depending on area that let them establish mortgage rates appropriately.

Value

This has probably already been underscored in the previous points, but the most important V that needs to be emphasized is the value of the data in big data systems. The best part about big data systems is that the value is not just one time. Data is gathered and stored assuming it is of value to different audiences. The value of data also changes over time, either turning irrelevant as trends change or showing patterns that have precedence in the past. Let's take the example of sales data. Sales data is used to drive revenue and tax calculations as well as to calculate the commissions of the sales employees. In addition, an analysis of the sales trends over time can be used to project future trends and set sales targets. Applying machine learning techniques on sales data and correlating it with seemingly unrelated data, such as social media trends or weather data, can predict unique trends in sales. One important thing to remember is that the value of data has the potential to depreciate over time, depending on the problem you are trying to solve. As an example, the dataset containing weather patterns across the globe has a lot of value if you are analyzing how climate trends are changing over time. However, if you are trying to predict umbrella sales patterns, then the weather patterns from five years ago are less relevant.

Figure 1-2 illustrates these concepts of big data.

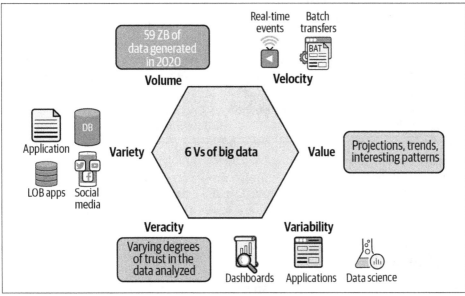

Figure 1-2. Six Vs of big data

Elastic Data Infrastructure—The Challenge

For organizations to realize the value of data, the infrastructure for storing, processing, and analyzing data while scaling to the growing demands of volume and the format diversity becomes critical. This infrastructure must have the capabilities not just to store data of any format, size, and shape but also to ingest, process, and consume this large variety of data to extract valuable insights.

In addition, this infrastructure needs to keep up with the proliferation of the data and its growing variety and be able to scale elastically as the needs of the organizations grow and the demand for data and insights increases.

Cloud Computing Fundamentals

Terms such as *cloud computing* and *elastic infrastructure* are so ubiquitous today that they have become part of our natural language, just like "Ask Siri" or "Did you Google that?" While we don't pause for a second when we hear or use these terms, what do they mean, and why are they the biggest trendsetters for transformation? Let's get our head in the clouds for a bit here and learn about cloud computing fundamentals before we dive into cloud data lakes.

Cloud computing is a big shift from how organizations traditionally thought about IT resources. In a traditional approach, organizations had IT departments that purchased devices or appliances to run software. These devices were either laptops or desktops that were provided to developers and information workers, or they were datacenters that IT departments maintained and provided access to the rest of the organization. IT departments had budgets to procure hardware and managed the support with the hardware vendors. They also had operational procedures and associated labor provisioned to install and update the operating systems and software that ran on this hardware. This posed a few problems: business continuity was threatened by hardware failures, software development and usage were blocked by having limited resources available from a small IT department to manage installation and upgrades, and most important, there wasn't a way to scale the hardware, which impeded the growth of the business.

Cloud Computing Terminology

Very simply put, cloud computing can be understood as having your IT department deliver computing resources over the internet. The cloud computing resources themselves are owned, operated, and maintained by a cloud provider. Cloud is not homogenous—there are different types of clouds as well:

Public cloud

Public cloud providers include Microsoft Azure, Amazon Web Services (AWS), and Google Cloud Platform (GCP), to name a few. The public cloud providers own datacenters that host racks and racks of computers in regions across the world, and they can have computing resources from different organizations leveraging the same set of infrastructure, called a *multitenant system*. The public cloud providers offer guarantees of isolation to ensure that while different organizations can use the same infrastructure, one organization cannot access another organization's resources.

Private cloud

Providers such as VMware offer private clouds, where the computing resources are hosted in on-premises datacenters that are entirely dedicated to an organization. As an analogy, think of a public cloud provider as a strip mall, which can host sandwich shops, bakeries, dentist offices, music classes, and hair salons in the same physical building. On the other hand, a private cloud is like a school building where the entire building is used only for the school. Public cloud providers also offer private cloud versions of their services.

Your organization could use more than one cloud provider to meet your needs, referred to as a *multicloud* approach. On the other hand, some organizations opt for what is called a *hybrid cloud*, where they have a private cloud on an on-premises infrastructure and leverage a public cloud service, and their resources move between the two environments as needed. Figure 1-3 illustrates these concepts.

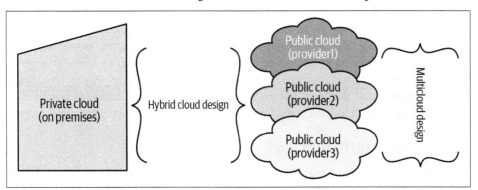

Figure 1-3. Cloud concepts

We talked about computing resources, but what exactly are these? Computing resources on the cloud belong to three different categories:

Infrastructure as a service, or IaaS

For any offering, there needs to be a barebones infrastructure that consists of resources that offer compute (processing), storage (data), and networking (connectivity). IaaS offerings refer to virtualized compute, storage, and networking resources that you can create on the public cloud to build your own service or solution leveraging these resources.

Platform as a service, or PaaS

PaaS resources are essentially tools that providers offer, which application developers can leverage to build their own solutions. These PaaS resources could be provided by the public cloud providers or providers that exclusively offer these tools. Some examples of PaaS resources are operational databases offered as a service, such as Microsoft's Azure Cosmos DB, Amazon's Redshift, Atlas's MongoDB, or Snowflake's data warehouse, which builds this as a service on all public clouds.

Software as a service, or SaaS

SaaS resources offer ready-to-use software services for a subscription. You can use them anywhere with nothing to install on your computers, and while you could leverage your developers to customize the solutions, there are out-of-the-box capabilities that you can start using right away. Some examples of SaaS services are Microsoft 365, Netflix, Salesforce, and Adobe Creative Cloud.

As an analogy, let's say you want to eat pizza for dinner. If you were leveraging IaaS, you would buy flour, yeast, cheese, and vegetables and make your own dough, add toppings, and bake your pizza. You need to be an expert cook to do this right. If you were leveraging PaaS, you would buy a take-and-bake pizza and pop it into your oven. You don't need to be an expert cook; however, you need to know enough to operate an oven and watch out to ensure the pizza is not burned. If you were using SaaS, you would call the local pizza shop and have the pizza delivered hot to your house. You don't need to have any cooking expertise, and you have pizza ready to eat.

Value Proposition of the Cloud

One of the first questions that I always get from customers and organizations taking their first steps on their cloud journey is why move to the cloud in the first place. Although the return on investment could be multifold, the value can be divided into three key categories:

Lowered TCO

TCO refers to the total cost of ownership of the technical solution you maintain, including the datacenter costs, the software costs, and the salaries of people who need to be employed to manage the operations. In almost all cases, barring a few exceptions, the TCO is significantly lower for building solutions on the cloud compared with the solutions that are built in house and deployed in your on-premises datacenter. This is because you can focus on hiring software teams to write code for your business logic while the cloud providers take care of all other hardware and software needs for you. Some of the contributors to this lowered cost include the following:

Cost of hardware

The cloud providers own, build, and support the hardware resources at a lower cost than if you were to build and run your own datacenters, maintain hardware, and renew your hardware when the support runs out. Further, with the advances made in hardware, cloud providers enable newer hardware to be accessible much faster than if you were to build your own datacenters.

Cost of software

In addition to building and maintaining hardware, one of the key efforts for an IT organization is to support and deploy operating systems and keep them updated. Typically, these updates involve planned downtimes that can also be disruptive to your organization. The cloud providers take care of this cycle without burdening your IT department. In almost all cases, these updates happen in an abstracted fashion so that you don't need to be affected by any downtime.

Pay for what you use

Most of the cloud services work on a subscription-based billing model, which means that you pay for what you use. If you have resources that are used for certain hours of the day or certain days of the week, you only pay for that time, which is a lot less expensive than having hardware all the time even if you don't use it.

Elastic scale

The resources that you need for your business are highly dynamic in nature, and there are times when you need to provision resources for planned and unplanned increases in usage. When you maintain and run your hardware, you are tied to the hardware you have as the ceiling for the growth you can support in your business. Cloud resources have an elastic scale, and you can burst into high demand by leveraging additional resources in a few clicks.

Ability to keep up with innovations

Cloud providers are constantly innovating and adding new services and technologies to their offerings depending on what they learn from multiple customers. Leveraging state-of-the-art services and technologies helps you innovate faster for your business scenarios, compared with having in-house developers who might not have the necessary breadth of knowledge across the industry.

Cloud Data Lake Architecture

To understand how cloud data lakes help with the growing data needs of an organization, it's important for us to first understand how data processing and insights worked a few decades ago. Businesses often thought of data as something that supplemented a business problem that needed to be solved. The approach was business problem–centric and involved the following steps:

1. Identify the problem to be solved.
2. Define a structure for data that can help solve the problem.
3. Collect or generate the data that adheres with the structure.
4. Store the data in an OLTP database, such as Microsoft SQL Server.
5. Use another set of transformations (filtering, aggregations, etc.) to store data in OLAP databases; SQL servers are used here as well.
6. Build dashboards and queries from these OLAP databases to solve your business problem.

For instance, when an organization wanted to understand sales, it built an application for salespeople to input their leads, customers, and engagements along with the sales data, and this application was supported by one or more operational databases. There could be one database storing customer information, another storing employee information for the sales force, and a third that stored the sales information referencing both the customer and employee databases. On premises (referred to as "on prem") has three layers, as shown in Figure 1-4:

Enterprise data warehouse
> This is the component where the data is stored. It contains a database component to store the data and a metadata component to describe the data stored in the database.

Data marts
> Data marts are a segment of the enterprise data warehouse that contain business- or topic-focused databases that have data ready to serve the application. Data in the warehouse goes through another set of transformations to be stored in the data marts.

Consumption/business intelligence (BI) layer
> This consists of the various visualization and query tools used by BI analysts to query the data in the data marts (or the warehouse) to generate insights.

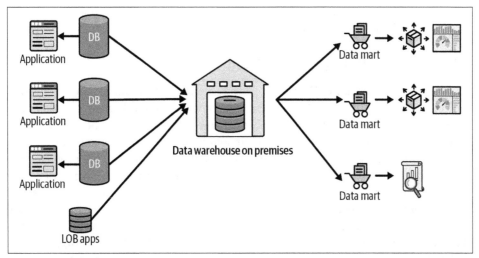

Figure 1-4. Traditional on-premises data warehouse

Limitations of On-Premises Data Warehouse Solutions

While this works well for providing insights into the business, there are a few key limitations with this architecture:

Highly structured data

This architecture expects data to be highly structured every step of the way. As we saw in the previous examples, this assumption is not realistic anymore; data can come from any source, such as IoT sensors, social media feeds, and video/audio files, and it can be any format (JSON, CSV, PNG—fill this list with all the formats you know). In most cases, a strict structure cannot be enforced.

Siloed data stores

Multiple copies of the same data are stored in data stores that are specialized for specific purposes. This proves to be a disadvantage because there is a high cost for storing these copies of the same data, and the process of copying data back and forth is both expensive and error prone, resulting in inconsistent versions of data across multiple data stores while the data is being copied.

Hardware provisioning for peak utilization

On-premises data warehouses require organizations to install and maintain the hardware required to run these services. When you expect bursts in demand (think of budget closing for the fiscal year or projecting more sales over the holidays), you need to plan ahead for this peak utilization and buy the hardware, even if it means that some of your hardware will lie around underutilized for the rest of the time. This increases your TCO. Note that this is specifically a limitation with respect to on-premises hardware rather than a difference between data warehouse and data lake architecture.

What Is a Cloud Data Lake Architecture?

As we saw in "What Is Big Data?" on page 2, the big data scenarios go way beyond the confines of traditional enterprise data warehouses. Cloud data lake architectures are designed to solve these exact problems, since they were designed to meet the needs of explosive growth of data and their sources without making any assumptions about the source, formats, size, or quality of the data. In contrast to the problem-first approach taken by traditional data warehouses, cloud data lakes take a data-first approach. In a cloud data lake architecture, all data is considered to be useful—either immediately or to meet a future need. The first step in a cloud data architecture involves ingesting data in its raw, natural state, without any restrictions on the source, size, or format of the data. This data is stored in a cloud data lake, a storage system that is highly scalable and can store any kind of data. This raw data has variable quality and value and needs more transformations to generate high-value insights.

As shown in Figure 1-5, the processing systems on a cloud data lake work on the data that is stored in the data lake and allow the data developer to define a schema on demand—that is, describe the data at the time of processing. These processing systems then operate on the low-value unstructured data to generate high-value data that is often structured and contains meaningful insights. This high-value, structured data is then either loaded into an enterprise data warehouse for consumption or consumed directly from the data lake. If all these concepts seem highly complex to understand, no worries—we will go into a lot of detail about this processing in Chapters 2 and 3.

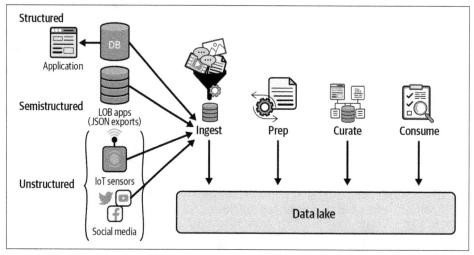

Figure 1-5. Cloud data lake architecture

Benefits of a Cloud Data Lake Architecture

At a high level, the cloud data lake architecture addresses limitations of the traditional data warehouse architectures in the following ways:

No restrictions on the data

As we saw, a data lake architecture consists of tools that are designed to ingest, store, and process all kinds of data without imposing any restrictions on the source, size, or structure of the data. In addition, these systems are designed to work with data that enters the data lake at any speed: real-time data emitted continuously as well as volumes of data ingested in batches on a scheduled basis. Further, the data lake storage is extremely low cost, so this lets us store all data by default without worrying about the bills. Remember how you would have once needed to think twice before taking pictures with those old film-roll cameras but these days click away without as much as a second thought with your phone camera.

Single storage layer with no silos

Note that in a cloud data lake architecture, your processing happens on data in the same store, so you don't need specialized data stores for specialized purposes anymore. This not only lowers your cost but also avoids errors involved in moving data back and forth across different storage systems.

Flexibility of running diverse compute on the same data store

As you can see, a cloud data lake architecture inherently decouples compute and storage, so while the storage layer serves as a no-silos repository, you can run a variety of data processing computational tools on the same storage layer. As an example, you can leverage the same data storage layer to do data-warehouse-like BI queries, advanced machine learning, and data science computations or even bespoke domain-specific computations, such as high-performance computing like media processing or analysis of seismic data.

Pay for what you use

Cloud services and tools are always designed to elastically scale up and down on demand, and you can create and delete processing systems on demand. This means that for those bursts in demand during the holiday season or budget closing, you can choose to spin these systems up without having them around for the rest of the year. This drastically reduces the TCO.

Independently scale compute and storage

In a cloud data lake architecture, compute and storage are different types of resources, and they can be independently scaled, thereby allowing you to scale your resources depending on need. Storage systems on the cloud are very cheap and enable you to store a large amount of data without breaking the bank.

Compute resources are traditionally more expensive than storage; however, they can be started or stopped on demand, thereby offering economy at scale.

 Technically, it is possible to scale compute and storage independently in an on-premises Apache Hadoop architecture as well. However, this involves careful consideration of hardware choices that are optimized specifically for compute and storage and have an optimized network connectivity. This is exactly what cloud providers offer with their cloud infrastructure services. Very few organizations have this kind of expertise and explicitly choose to run their services on premises.

This flexibility of processing all kinds of data in a cost-efficient fashion helps organizations realize the value of data and turn data into valuable transformational insights.

Defining Your Cloud Data Lake Journey

I have talked to hundreds of customers about their big data analytics scenarios and helped them with parts of their cloud data lake journeys. These customers have different motivations and problems to solve: some customers are new to the cloud and want to take their first steps with data lakes, others have a data lake implemented on the cloud supporting some basic scenarios and are not sure what to do next, some are cloud native customers who want to start right with data lakes as part of their application architectures, and others already have a mature implementation of their data lakes on the cloud and want to harness the power of data to offer the next level of differentiated value compared to their peers and competitors. If I had to summarize my learnings from all these conversations, it basically comes down to two key things:

- Regardless of your cloud maturity level, design your data lake for the company's future.
- Make your implementation choices based on what you need immediately!

You may be thinking that this sounds too obvious and too generic. However, in the rest of the book, you will observe that the framework and guidance I prescribe for designing and optimizing cloud data lakes are going to assume that you are constantly checkpointing yourself against these two questions:

1. What is the business problem driving the decisions on the data lake?
2. When I solve this problem, what else can I be doing to differentiate my business with the data lake?

Let me give you a concrete example. A common scenario that drives customers to implement a cloud data lake is that their on-premises hardware supporting their Hadoop cluster is nearing its end of life. This Hadoop cluster is primarily used by the data platform and BI teams to build dashboards and cubes with data ingested from their on-premises transactional storage systems, and the company needs to decide whether to buy more hardware and continue maintaining their on-premises hardware or to invest in this cloud data lake that everyone keeps talking about, where the promise is elastic scale, lower cost of ownership, a larger set of features and services they can leverage, and all the other goodness we saw in the previous section. When these customers decide to move to the cloud, they have a ticking clock that they need to respect when their hardware reaches its end of life, so they pick a lift-and-shift strategy that takes their existing on-premises implementation and ports it to the cloud. This is a perfectly fine approach, especially given that these are production systems that serve a critical business function. However, three things these customers soon realize are as follows:

- It takes a lot of effort to even lift and shift their implementation.
- If they realize the value of the cloud and want to add more scenarios, they are constrained by their design choices, such as security models, data organization, and so on, which originally assumed one set of BI scenarios running on the data lake.
- In some instances, lift-and-shift architectures end up being more expensive in terms of both cost and maintenance, negating the original purpose.

Well, that's surprising, isn't it? These surprises primarily stem from the differences in architectures between on-premises and cloud systems. In an on-premises Hadoop cluster, compute and storage are colocated and tightly coupled, whereas on the cloud, the idea is to have an object storage/data lake storage layer, such as Amazon S3, Azure Data Lake Store (ADLS), and Google Cloud Storage (GCS), and have a plethora of compute options available as either IaaS (provision VMs and run your own software) or PaaS (e.g., Azure HDInsight, Amazon EMR, etc.), as shown in Figure 1-6. On the cloud, your data lake solution essentially is a structure you build out of Lego pieces, which could be IaaS, PaaS, or SaaS offerings.

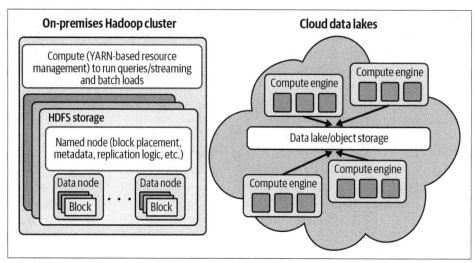

Figure 1-6. On-premises versus cloud architectures

We already saw the advantages of decoupled compute and storage architectures in terms of independent scaling and lowered cost; however, this requires that the architecture and design of your cloud data lake respects this decoupled architecture. For example, in the cloud data lake implementation, the compute systems talk to the storage systems over the networking systems, as opposed to local calls. If you do not optimize this, both your cost and performance are affected. Similarly, once you have completed your data lake implementation for your primary BI scenarios, you can now get more value out of your data lake by enabling more scenarios, bringing in disparate datasets, or conducting more data science exploratory analysis on the data in your lake. At the same time, you want to make sure that a data science exploratory job does not accidentally delete your datasets that power the dashboard that your VP of sales wants to see every morning. You need to ensure that the data organization and security models you have in place ensure this isolation and access control.

Tying these amazing opportunities back with the original motivation you had to move to the cloud, which was your on-premises servers reaching their end of life, you need to formulate a plan that helps you meet your timelines while setting you up for success on the cloud. Your move to the cloud data lake involves two goals:

- Shutting down your on-premises systems
- Setting you up for success on the cloud

Most customers end up focusing only on the first goal and drive themselves into huge technical debt before they have to rearchitect their applications. When you think about a cloud data lake architecture, ensure that you have the following as your goal post:

- Migrate your data lake to the cloud.
- Modernize your data lake to suit the cloud architecture.

These two goals will go hand in hand in helping you identify an architecture that is robust to the growing scale and needs of your business.

To understand how to achieve both of these goals, you will need to understand what the cloud architecture is, what the design considerations for implementation are, and how to optimize your data lake for scale and performance. We will address these questions in detail in Chapters 2–4. We will also focus on providing a framework that helps you consider the various aspects of your cloud data lake journey.

Summary

In this chapter, we started off talking about the value proposition of data and the transformational insights that can turn organizations around. We also built a fundamental understanding of cloud computing and the differences between a traditional data warehouse and a cloud data lake architecture. Finally, we looked at what big data, the cloud, and data lakes are. Given the difference between on-premises and cloud architectures, we emphasized the importance of a mindset shift that in turn defines an architecture shift when designing a cloud data lake. This mindset change is the one thing I would implore you to make as we delve into the details of cloud data lake architectures and their implementation considerations in the next chapters.

CHAPTER 2

Big Data Architectures on the Cloud

Big data may mean more information, but it also means more false information.

—Naseem Taleb

As we learned in Chapter 1, there are two key takeaways about cloud data lakes that set the foundation for this chapter:

- A data lake approach starts with the ability to store and process any type of data regardless of its source, size, or structure, thereby allowing an organization to extract high-value insights from many disparate sources of data with variable value density (i.e., signal-to-noise ratio).

- Building your data lake on the cloud involves a disaggregated architecture where you assemble different components of IaaS, PaaS, and SaaS solutions together.

What is important to remember is that building your cloud data lake solution also gives you a lot of options for architectures, each with its own set of strengths. This article on Future.com (*https://oreil.ly/VUHSK*) provides a comprehensive overview of the various components of a modern data architecture. In this chapter, we will dive deep into some of the more common architectural patterns, covering what they are as well as understanding the strengths of each of these architectures as they apply to a fictitious organization called Klodars Corporation.

Why Klodars Corporation Moves to the Cloud

Klodars Corporation is a thriving company that sells rain gear and other supplies in the Pacific Northwest region. The rapid growth in its business is driving its move to the cloud for the following reasons:

- The databases running on the on-premises systems do not scale anymore to the rapid growth of the business.

- As the business grows, the team is growing too. Both the sales and marketing teams are observing that their applications are getting a lot slower and even timing out sometimes because of the increasing number of users concurrently using the system.

- The marketing department wants more input into how it can best target its campaigns on social media and is exploring the idea of leveraging influencers but doesn't know how or where to start.

- The sales department cannot rapidly expand work with customers distributed across three states, so it is struggling to prioritize the kinds of retail customers and wholesale distributors it wants to engage first.

- The investors love the growth of the business and are asking the CEO how Klodars Corporation can expand beyond winter gear. The CEO needs to figure out the expansion strategy.

Alice, a motivated leader from the software development team, pitches to the CEO and CTO of Klodars Corporation the idea of looking into the cloud and seeing how other business are leveraging a data lake approach to solve the challenges they are experiencing. She also gathers data points that show the opportunities that a cloud data lake approach can present, including the following:

- The cloud can scale elastically to the company's growing needs, and given that it pays for consumption, it doesn't need to overprovision its hardware to budget for peak seasons and have the hardware sit around at other times.

- Cloud-based data lakes and data warehouses can scale to support the growing number of concurrent users.

- The cloud data lake has tools and services to process data from various sources, such as website clickstreams, retail analytics, social media feeds, and even the weather, so the company can have a better understanding of its marketing campaigns.

- Klodars Corporation can hire data analysts and data scientists to process trends from the market to help provide valuable signals to help with its expansion strategy.

The CEO is completely sold on this approach and wants to try out the cloud data lake solution. At this point in its journey, it's important for Klodars Corporation to keep its existing business running while it starts experimenting with the cloud approach. Let's take a look at how different cloud architectures can bring unique strengths to Klodars while also helping meet its needs arising from rapid growth and expansion.

Fundamentals of Cloud Data Lake Architectures

Prior to deploying a cloud data lake architecture, it's important to understand that there are four key components that create the foundation and serve as building blocks for the cloud data lake architecture. These are the components:

- The data itself
- The data lake storage
- The big data analytics engines that process the data
- The cloud data warehouse

A Word on Variety of Data

We have already mentioned that data lakes support a variety of data, but what does this variety actually mean? Let's take the example of the data we talked about previously, specifically the inventory and sales datasets. Logically speaking, this data is tabular in nature, which means that it consists of rows and columns that can be represented in a table. However, in reality, how this tabular data is represented depends on the source that is generating the data. Roughly speaking, there are three broad categories of data when it comes to big data processing:

Structured data
    This refers to a set of formats where the data resides in a defined structure (rows and columns) and adheres to a predefined schema that is strictly enforced. A classic example is data that is found in relational databases like SQL, which would look something like what is shown in Figure 2-1. The data is stored in specialized custom-made binary formats for the relational databases and is optimized to store tabular data (data organized as rows and columns). These formats are proprietary and tailor-made for specific systems. The consumers of the data, whether they are users or applications, understand this structure and schema and rely on them to write their applications. Any data that does not adhere to the rules is discarded and not stored in the databases. The relational database engines

also store this data in an optimized binary format that is efficient to store and process.

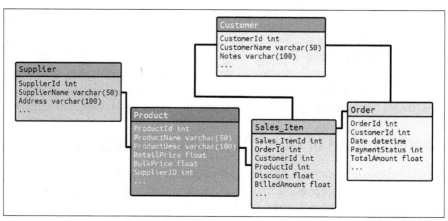

Figure 2-1. Structured data in databases

Semistructured data

This refers to a set of formats where there is a structure present; however, it is loosely defined and offers flexibility to customize the structure if needed. JSON and XML are examples of semistructured data. Figure 2-2 shows a representation of semistructured data of the sales item ID in two formats. The power of these semistructured data formats lies in their flexibility. Once you start designing a schema and then determine that you need some extra data, you can go ahead and store the data with extra fields without compromising any violation of structure. The existing engines that read the data will continue to work without disruption, and new engines can incorporate the new fields. Similarly, when different sources are sending similar data (e.g., point-of-sale systems and website telemetry can both send sales information), you can take advantage of the flexible schema to support those multiple sources.

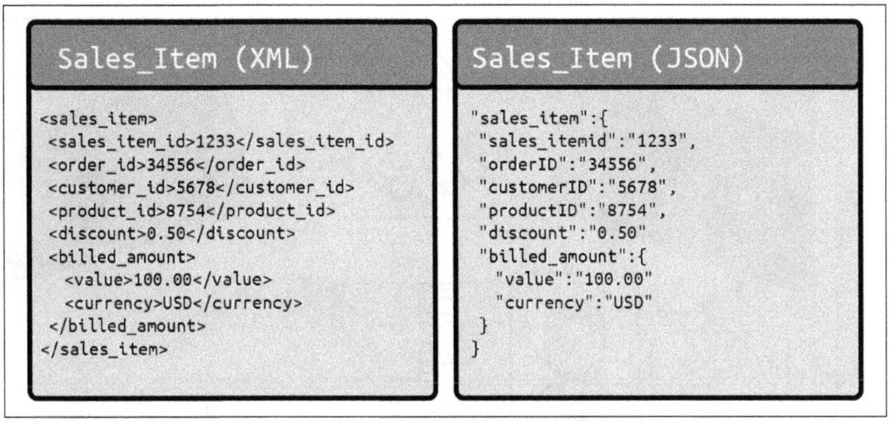

```
Sales_Item (XML)                       Sales_Item (JSON)

<sales_item>                           "sales_item":{
  <sales_item_id>1233</sales_item_id>    "sales_itemid":"1233",
  <order_id>34556</order_id>             "orderID":"34556",
  <customer_id>5678</customer_id>        "customerID":"5678",
  <product_id>8754</product_id>          "productID":"8754",
  <discount>0.50</discount>              "discount":"0.50"
  <billed_amount>                        "billed_amount":{
    <value>100.00</value>                  "value":"100.00"
    <currency>USD</currency>               "currency":"USD"
  </billed_amount>                       }
</sales_item>                          }
```

Figure 2-2. Semistructured data

Unstructured data

This refers to formats that have no restrictions on how data is stored, which could be as simple as a free-form note like a comment on a social media feed or as complex as an MPEG4 video or PDF document. Unstructured data is probably the toughest of the formats to process because it requires custom written parsers that can understand and extract the right information out of the data. At the same time, it is one of the easiest of the formats to store in general-purpose object storage because it has no restrictions whatsoever. For instance, think of a picture in a social media feed where the seller can tag an item and, once somebody purchases the item, add another tag saying it's sold. The processing engine needs to process the image to understand what item was sold and then process the labels to understand what the price was and who bought it. While this is not impossible, it takes a lot of effort to understand the data, and the quality is low because it relies on human tagging. However, this expands the horizons of flexibility into various avenues that can be used to make the sales. For example, you could write an engine to process pictures in social media to understand which realtor sold houses in a given area for what price, as shown in Figure 2-3.

Figure 2-3. Unstructured data

Cloud Data Lake Storage

The very simple definition of *cloud data lake storage* is a service available as a cloud offering that can serve as a central repository for all kinds of data (structured, unstructured, and semistructured) and can support data and transactions at a large scale. When I say "large scale," think of a storage system that supports storing hundreds of PBs of data and several hundred thousand transactions per second, and can keep elastically scaling as both data and transactions continue to grow. In most public cloud offerings, the data lake storage is available as a PaaS offering, also called an object storage service. Data lake storage services offer rich data management capabilities, such as tiered storage (different tiers have different costs associated with them, and you can move rarely used data to a lower cost tier), high availability and disaster recovery with various degrees of replication, and rich security models that allow the administrator to control access for various consumers. Let's take a look at some of the most popular cloud data lake storage offerings:

Amazon S3 (Simple Storage Service)
    S3 offered by Amazon is a large-scale object storage service and is recommended as the storage solution for building your data lake architecture on AWS. The entity stored in S3 (structured and unstructured datasets) is referred to as an *object*, and objects are organized into containers that are called *buckets*. S3

also enables users to organize their objects by grouping them together using a common prefix (think of this as a virtual directory). Administrators can control access to S3 by applying access policies at either the bucket or prefix levels. In addition, data operators can add tags, which are essentially key value pairs, to objects. These serve as labels or hashtags that let you retrieve objects by specifying the tags. Amazon S3 also offers rich data management features to manage the cost of the data, as well as increased security guarantees. To learn more about S3, you can visit the document page (*https://aws.amazon.com/s3*).

Azure Data Lake Storage (ADLS)

ADLS is a Microsoft Azure storage offering that provides a native filesystem with a hierarchical namespace on its general-purpose object storage service (Azure Blob storage). According to the ADLS product website (*https://oreil.ly/0nnWd*), ADLS is a single storage platform for ingestion, processing, and visualization that supports the most common analytics frameworks. You can provision a storage account, where you will specify Yes to "Enable Hierarchical Namespace" to create an ADLS account. ADLS offers a unit of organization called a *container* and a native file system with directories and files to organize the data. You can visit the document page (*https://oreil.ly/hG7ah*) to learn more about ADLS.

Google Cloud Storage (GCS)

GCS is offered by GCP as the object storage service and is recommended as the data lake storage solution. Similar to S3, data in Google is referred to as objects and is organized in buckets. You can learn more about GCS on the document page (*https://oreil.ly/DDuNH*).

Cloud data storage services have the capability to load data from a wide variety of sources, including on-premises storage solutions, and to integrate with real-time data ingestion services that connect to sources like IoT sensors. They also integrate with the on-premises systems and services that support legacy applications. In addition, a plethora of data processing engines can process the data stored in the data lake storage services. These data processing engines fall into many categories:

- PaaS solutions that are part of the public cloud offerings (e.g., EMR (*https://aws.amazon.com/emr*) by AWS, HDInsight (*https://oreil.ly/dQpCe*) and Azure Synapse Analytics (*https://oreil.ly/7GHE2*) by Azure, and Dataproc (*https://cloud.google.com/dataproc*) by GCP)

- PaaS solutions developed by other software companies, such as Databricks (*https://databricks.com*), Dremio (*https://www.dremio.com*), Talend (*https://talend.com*), Informatica (*https://informatica.com*), and Cloudera (*https://cloudera.com*)

- SaaS solutions, such as Microsoft Power BI (*https://powerbi.microsoft.com*), Tableau (*https://tableau.com*), and Looker (*https://looker.com*)

You can also provision IaaS solutions like VMs and run your own distro of software like Apache Spark to query the data lakes.

One important point to note is that the compute and storage are disaggregated in the data lake architecture, and you can run one or more of the processing engines on data in the data lake without having to move the data. Some of the popular data warehouses are Amazon Redshift, Google BigQuery, and Snowflake Data Cloud. The data warehouses offer both compute and storage, and while the data warehouses in some cases support querying data that resides in a separate data lake storage, the most common use case is to use the most optimized path: query the data that resides in the data warehouse in a proprietary data format. Recently, data warehouses have started supporting open data formats like Apache Iceberg, a very promising trend that directionally supports the data lakehouse architecture, which we will cover in more detail in this chapter as well.

Big Data Analytics Engines

At this point, we understand that big data analytics is the processing of structured, semistructured, and unstructured data. Now let's discover what this processing actually looks like. When we talk about big data analytics on the data lake, the processing that happens is most likely one of the following described here, or a derivative of them.

MapReduce

The origins of big data and analytics processing lies in the advent of something that changed how we work: *search engines*. Search engines largely work by crawling text data from all sources on the internet and building a humongous index of keywords that is mapped to web pages. When the user searches for a keyword, the search engine then ranks the data from this index and provides an ordered set of results to the user. While the design of search engines by itself warrants a book and is not something we will address here in detail, they demonstrated that there was a need to process large volumes of data that can be reduced to a searchable index, giving birth to a programming model called *MapReduce*.

MapReduce is essentially a programming model and associated implementation that takes an input set of key-value pairs and produces an output set of key-value pairs. Sounds simple, doesn't it? The issue here is scale—doing this transformation across a set of data that has millions and millions of records. As Jeffrey Dean and Sanjay Ghemawat describe in their paper "MapReduce: Simplified Data Processing on Large Clusters" (*https://research.google/pubs/pub62*), MapReduce has two phases, as the name suggests. In the map phase, data is organized by a key with a logic to group similar values together, resulting in an intermediate key-value pair. The reduce phase processes these similar datasets to produce a filtered set of results, again as a key-value pair.

As an example, let's take Twitter data, where the goal is to understand how many mentions there are for each user in a large set of feeds (a smaller sample is illustrated in Figure 2-4). There is a set of compute units at work here: multiple worker units that operate on a dataset assigned to them and a main orchestrator unit that does the coordination between the worker units. The compute units could be VMs, processes, or threads depending on the implementation. The large set of Twitter data feeds is broken down into smaller sets (in this example, one feed) and assigned to worker units, where they are mapping the mentions to counts and generating a set of output key-value pairs, as illustrated in Figure 2-4. These data values are then sent to another set of worker units to do a reduce to generate the count of mentions per user. The primary advantage is that this programming model lets the large dataset be effectively distributed across a large set of worker units with a predictable distribution mechanism.

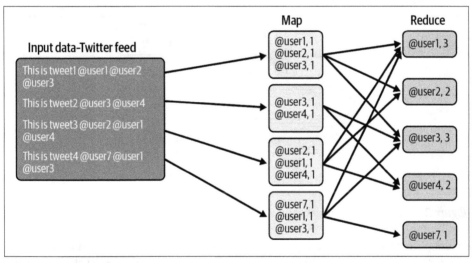

Figure 2-4. MapReduce

Apache Hadoop

Apache, an open source organization, had an open source web search project called Apache Nutch (*http://nutch.apache.org*), which is used even today. In 2005, as part of Apache Nutch, Doug Cutting and Mike Cafarella created Apache Hadoop (*https://hadoop.apache.org*), a set of tools, libraries, and components for distributed processing of large datasets that uses MapReduce as its core processing logic. Apache Hadoop consists of four primary components:

Hadoop Common Module
> A common set of libraries that supports other modules

Hadoop Distributed File System (HDFS)
> A distributed storage system for large datasets

Hadoop MapReduce
> A programming model and implementation for large-scale processing of large datasets

Hadoop YARN
> A framework for job scheduling and resource management to distribute work and data across a cluster of machines

Hadoop laid a strong foundation that birthed various other open source projects, such as Apache Hive, Apache Pig, Apache Storm, and Apache Mahout, to build more frameworks and programming models for distributed big data processing. A detailed index of all the Hadoop projects and tools is provided in this Hadoop Ecosystem Table (*https://oreil.ly/WGgSR*), and a sample is shown in Figure 2-5.

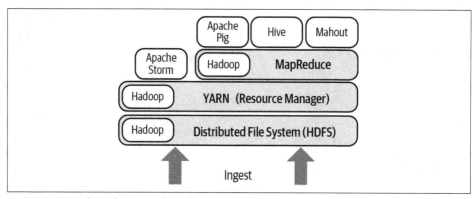

Figure 2-5. Hadoop framework and ecosystem

Hadoop commoditized the big data processing ecosystem, and vendors like Hortonworks and Cloudera sold their distributions of Hadoop that customers could install on premises or on the cloud. Public cloud providers also offer their packaged versions of Hadoop-based processing as PaaS solutions, such as Elastic MapReduce (EMR) by AWS and HDInsight by Microsoft Azure. With all of these different Hadoop-flavored offerings, you might wonder what to pick. While there are many reasons, such as familiarity with the vendor, sales and marketing relationships, and so on, a few technical key factors contribute to what a customer should choose:

- Customers who run on a hybrid environment, where they have both on-premises and cloud deployments, or run on a multicloud environment pick Hadoop offerings provided by independent software vendors (ISVs), such as Cloudera or Hortonworks, so their implementations work on all environments.

- Customers who prefer to have a tight integration of their big data platform with other native cloud services choose the offerings by the public cloud providers, such as AWS, Azure, and GCP.

- Customers who are willing to invest in a strong technical team and want to save on vendor costs make their own flavor of Hadoop by forking the open sourced repository and building their own platform.

This largely applies to other open source offerings like Apache Spark as well.

It would be fair to say that Hadoop laid the foundations of a data lake architecture by providing a comprehensive set of tools for processing big data, including MapReduce for batch processing, Apache Storm for real-time processing, and Apache Hive for querying data over a Hadoop architecture.

Apache Spark

Apache Spark (*https://spark.apache.org*) was incubated at the AMPLab (*https://amplab.cs.berkeley.edu*) at the University of California, Berkeley, which focuses on big data analytics. The goal of Apache Spark is to provide a flexible programming model that has the fault tolerance and scale of MapReduce for distributed data processing while also supporting a wider variety of applications, such as machine learning, that rely on iterative processing of data and real-time processing that offers instant insights.

Like Hadoop, Spark uses an underlying storage layer; however, there is no mandate that this needs to be an HDFS storage; cloud object storage services or even local storage is supported by Spark. Similarly, Spark uses a cluster manager, and again, various options are supported, such as YARN (birthed from Hadoop) and Apache Mesos, which was also incubated at the University of California, Berkeley. Recently, given the rising popularity of Kubernetes and containers (simply defined as a ready-to-run software package that has your code, application runtimes, and any other components required to run your code) in cloud native development, Spark on Kubernetes (*https://oreil.ly/Ck4pd*) is gaining wide adoption as well. The key differentiator for Spark is the Spark core engine, which is built on a foundational abstraction of datasets as Resilient Distributed Datasets (RDDs) (*https://oreil.ly/tb5Y3*) without having to store the intermediate datasets to a persistent storage and still maintain fault tolerance. This model greatly increased the performance of Spark-based applications and offered a unified programming model for batch processing, interactive queries (Spark SQL), data science (MLlib), real-time processing (Spark Streaming), and the recently introduced graph processing (GraphX). The ease of use and the increasing mindshare of Apache Spark helped commoditize big data processing across various industries. You can either use Spark as its own distribution or leverage

Spark offered by public cloud providers (such as Amazon EMR, Azure Synapse Analytics, or Google Cloud Dataproc) or by software providers like Databricks, a company started by the inventors of Spark.

Figure 2-6 demonstrates the various technical components of Spark and how they layer on top of one another to provide a consistent programming model across machine learning, real time, and batch streaming.

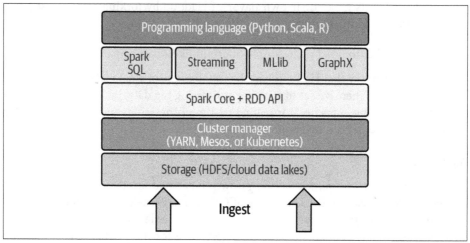

Figure 2-6. Apache Spark

Real-time stream processing pipelines

Real-time stream processing refers to the ingestion, processing, and consumption of data with a specific focus on speed, targeting near real time—that is, almost instantaneous results. Think of a time when you were traveling and you got a real-time notification from your favorite food review app about restaurants close to you that you could explore. There is a real-time processing pipeline at work that captures signals about your location from your mobile device and factors those with your profile and other related data to provide personalized recommendations in real time. Another example is the navigation app on your phone suggesting a different way when there is traffic on your regular route. In that case, there is a real-time processing pipeline that combines the real-time traffic data with the maps to suggest an optimal route to your destination.

Real-time stream processing pipelines involve data that is arriving from its source at *very high velocity*; in other words, it is data that is streaming into the system, just like rain or a waterfall. This could be data that is streaming from sources like GPS continuously, or it could be events that are emitted by IoT sensors, such as your home automation system or industrial devices. This data tends to be very small, typically a few kilobytes (KBs).

The processing part of real-time streaming pipelines involves processing the real-time streaming data, sometimes by combining it with other data that may not be real time, with a focus on low latency, typically in milliseconds. The typical scenario of a real-time processing application is to drive near-real-time insights so the consumer can take quick action, such as a system that processes the system logs and raises real-time alerts when there is an issue.

Real-time data processing technologies factor in the following aspects while processing data that is entering the system at high velocity and throughput:

Delivery guarantees
Real-time stream processing technologies offer delivery guarantees that determine how the real-time data will be processed. An at-least-once guarantee ensures that data coming in will be processed at least once and possibly multiple times to handle failures. An at-most-once guarantee ensures that data coming in will be processed at most once, avoiding duplicate processing. An exactly-once guarantee that ensures data will be processed exactly once is highly desired but also very difficult to achieve.

Fault tolerance
Real-time stream processing techniques need to ensure that they are resilient in case of failures, either in the cluster or in the underlying infrastructure, and are able to pick up where they left off.

State processing
Real-time stream processing frameworks offer state management: a record of how many messages were processed or what the last message processed was.

Real-time streaming data can be consumed in many ways: visualizations that demonstrate trends like social media trending charts, alerting systems such as security-incident detection, or even intelligent application behavior such as real-time recommendations based on your browsing patterns.

Figure 2-7 illustrates the architecture of a real-time streaming data pipeline. There are also multiple technologies available for you to build your real-time data pipelines. Apache Kafka (*https://kafka.apache.org*) is a prominent technology used for ingestion and storage of real-time streaming data that offers high throughput and scalability. Amazon Kinesis (*https://aws.amazon.com/kinesis*) and Azure Event Hub (*https://oreil.ly/jwp65*) are cloud native PaaS offerings that are built based on Apache Kafka as the underpinning technology. Apache Storm (*https://storm.apache.org*) and Apache Flink (*https://flink.apache.org*) are popular open source technologies that offer real-time data processing technologies. Apache Kafka also offers Kafka streams for real-time stream processing.

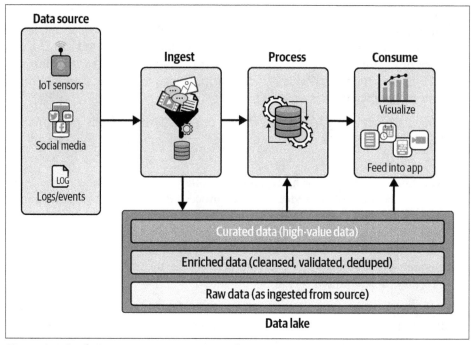

Figure 2-7. Real-time stream processing pipelines

Cloud Data Warehouses

A *cloud data warehouse* is an enterprise data warehouse offered as a managed service (PaaS) on public clouds with optimized integrations for data ingestion, analytics processing, and BI analytics. *BI analytics* refers to tools that support visualization and interactive querying capabilities. Cloud data warehouse offerings are designed to elastically scale with the customer's growing needs by abstracting the infrastructure away from the user, and they promise faster performance and lower cost of ownership than traditional on-premises data warehouses. Let's take a look at some of the most popular cloud data warehouse offerings:

Amazon Redshift

Amazon Redshift was the first popular cloud data warehouse offering on the public cloud. You can provision a Redshift cluster, where you can specify the number of compute nodes that you want. The cluster can support data at PB scale according to the product documentation. You can use PostgreSQL, a popular query language, to query data in your Redshift cluster. To learn more about Redshift, you can visit the product page (*https://aws.amazon.com/pm/redshift*). Redshift also announced the capability to share data across different Redshift clusters without copying data to promote sharing of data and insights (*https:// oreil.ly/unEUs*).

Google BigQuery

Unlike Redshift, where you provision your data warehouse as a cluster, Google BigQuery is a completely serverless, highly scalable data warehouse solution that abstracts the details of cluster management completely away from the customer. In addition, BigQuery has features like BigQuery Omni (*https://oreil.ly/ccsBP*) that allow you to use the BigQuery compute service across other clouds, such as AWS and Azure. To learn more about BigQuery, visit the product page (*https://oreil.ly/i8rtT*).

Azure Synapse Analytics

Azure Synapse Analytics is offered as a unified analytics platform on Microsoft Azure. Similar to Redshift, you can provision a data warehouse cluster and specify the number of nodes you want for your scenarios. You can also provision a Spark cluster for analytics scenarios in the same experience. In addition, you can run serverless queries in SQL or Spark. With serverless queries, you can simply submit a job without provisioning a cluster, similar to BigQuery. Azure Synapse Analytics also offers integrations in the same experience with other Azure services, such as Azure Machine Learning, Azure Cognitive Services, and Power BI. To learn more about Azure Synapse Analytics, visit the product page (*https://oreil.ly/oO8jg*).

Snowflake Data Cloud

Snowflake data warehouse is a managed data warehouse solution that is available on all public clouds—AWS, Amazon, and GCP. Designed as a truly scalable solution, Snowflake is offered as a single service, while the implementation runs on a disaggregated compute and storage architecture, making it highly scalable in the compute or storage dimension without compounding the cost. This disaggregation also lets you spin up different virtual warehouses that can access the same data, providing isolation between your different query scenarios. Snowflake also offers data sharing at a table and object level to other Snowflake accounts. To read more about Snowflake, visit the product page (*https://oreil.ly/gKddO*).

In this section, I presented a high-level overview of the concepts of the four components of a cloud data lake architecture: the data, the data lake storage, the compute engines, and the cloud data warehouse. I also provided an overview of the commonly used services and technologies, along with links for you to explore deeper. In the next section, I will go over cloud data lake architectures that represent different ways in which these building blocks can be assembled in a solution. As we are reading this book, rapid innovations are being made in both the data lake and the data warehouse offerings, blurring the boundaries between them. We will address this further in the data lakehouse architecture pattern.

Data in the cloud data lake architecture can serve many purposes. However, there are two major scenarios that are common consumption patterns in an organization:

Business intelligence
> Data is used by BI analysts to create dashboards or work on interactive queries to answer key business problems that are well defined and work on highly structured data.

Data science and machine learning
> Data is used by data scientists and machine learning engineers to do exploratory analysis and experimental work to answer complex problems that don't have a defined ruleset and require multiple iterations to get better. The data involved here assumes no structure.

Modern Data Warehouse Architecture

In a modern data warehouse architecture, both the data lake and the data warehouse peacefully coexist, each serving a distinct purpose. The data lake serves as low-cost storage for a large amount of data and supports exploratory scenarios such as data science and machine learning. The data warehouse stores high-value data and powers dashboards used by the business. It is also used by BI users to query the highly structured data to gain insights about the business.

Reference Architecture

Data is first ingested into a data lake from various sources: on-premises databases, social media feeds, and so on. This data is then transformed using big data analytics frameworks like Hadoop and Spark, where multiple datasets can be aggregated and filtered to generate high-value structured data. This data is then loaded into a cloud data warehouse to power dashboards, including interactive dashboards for BI analysts using their very familiar tool of choice—SQL. In addition, the data lake empowers a whole new set of scenarios that involve exploratory analysis by data scientists as well as machine learning models that can be fed back into their applications. A simplified representation of the modern data warehouse architecture is shown in Figure 2-8.

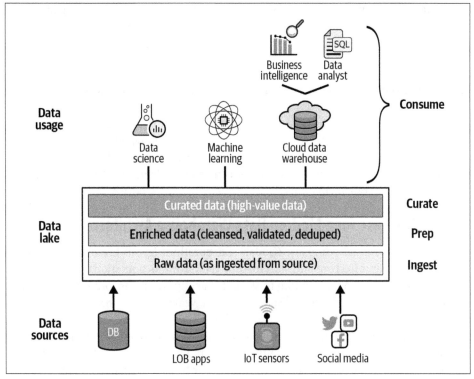

Figure 2-8. Modern data warehouse architecture

Some questions you would naturally ask here are: why not use a cloud data warehouse directly? Why is a data lake necessary in between? If I only have structured data, do I even need a data lake? If I may say so myself, these are great questions. There are a few reasons why you would need a data lake in this architecture:

- Data lakes cost a lot less than a data warehouse and can act as your long-term repository of data. Remember that data lakes are typically used to store large volumes of data (think tens or hundreds of PBs), so the difference in cost is material.

- Data lakes support a variety of modern tools and frameworks around data science and machine learning that you can use to enable completely new scenarios.

- Data lakes let you future-proof your design to scale to your growing needs. As an example, you might use your initial data lake architecture to load data from your on-premises systems on a nightly basis and publish reports or dashboards for your BI users. This same architecture is extensible to support real-time data ingestion without having to rearchitect your solution.

- Data of all forms and structures is largely becoming relevant to organizations. Even if you are focused on structured data today, as you saw in the previous example, you may find value in all kinds of data, such as weather, social media feeds, and the like.

In case you didn't observe this already, there is a difference in usage patterns that you need to remember: when you load data into a data warehouse, you use an *extract, transform, and load (ETL) pattern*, where you extract data from the source and transform the data to the format respected by the data warehouse before loading it into the data warehouse. In a data lake, you follow an *extract, load, and transform (ELT) pattern*, where you extract data from the source, load into the data lake as is, and then do your transformations.

Sample Use Case for a Modern Data Warehouse Architecture

Let's revisit our model company, Klodars Corporation. It will leverage the modern data warehouse architecture and start loading data from its operational databases into the data lake. Instead of continuing to store its backups on its on-premises systems, it can now create daily backups and store up to one year's worth of backups (or more if it wants to) in its data lake. Klodars can do this while the operational databases on its servers continue to serve their existing applications, thereby ensuring the continuity of the company's operations. In addition, Klodars will plan to load data from social media feeds that relate to rain gear and winter gear to analyze patterns. This architecture will also enable the company to load other data, such as its clickstream, into the data lake storage in real time using real-time ingestion techniques like Apache Kafka.

With the dataset up and ready to go, the data engineering team will use tools like Apache Spark to process the structured data from its database dumps and from the website clickstream to generate high-value data that shows the shopping and sales trends over time. The team will also process the social media feeds and extract data that pertains to rain gear and winter gear as well as any associated purchases that the same feeds indicate. This architecture will enable the data engineering team to generate high-value data on a scheduled basis (e.g., daily) on sales trends, inventory and supply, website-browsing trends, and social media trends around rain and winter gear. This data will then be loaded into the data warehouse and refreshed on a periodic basis (e.g., daily).

The data stored in the data warehouse is very high-value structured data. The business analysts will use this high-value data to build dashboards that show the sales trends quarter over quarter or month over month, so the sales teams can understand the trend of their sales and set projections for the upcoming time period. The business analysts can also slice and dice the data by factors like region, salespeople coverage, partners, and other attributes, so the leadership team can understand the growth drivers and make data-informed decisions about the company's expansion strategy. The marketing team consumes the social media and website-browsing trends by running interactive queries on the data warehouse to understand the next set of targeted marketing campaigns to develop. The team can also understand the impact of its marketing campaigns by correlating the campaigns with the sales results.

The impact doesn't stop there. Klodars now has formed a data science team that can build on the existing datasets, such as sales, social media trends, and website-browsing trends, to find interesting correlations and effects of influencers that are not straightforward to process with manual analysis. The team can bring additional datasets to the data lake, such as weather data, data about winter activities like skiing, and so on, to surface interesting insights to the leadership team. This data can be fed back to the data engineering team to be loaded into the warehouse to be consumed by the leadership, marketing, and sales teams.

Figure 2-9 provides a representation of the modern data warehouse architecture at Klodars Corporation.

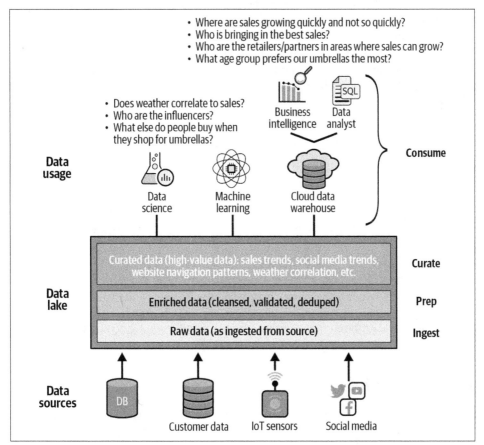

Figure 2-9. How Klodars Corporation leverages the modern data warehouse architecture

With the data lake strategy relying on a modern data warehouse architecture, Klodars Corporation is able to scale to its growing customer needs by prioritizing the right set of focus areas informed by data. Its modern data warehouse strategy enables the company to work on innovations while simultaneously keeping its existing business running. The phased movement of its existing applications to the modernized cloud architectures gives the team time to thoughtfully design and implement this transition.

Benefits and Challenges of Modern Data Warehouse Architecture

The modern data warehouse has an important benefit of helping the business analysts leverage familiar BI tool sets (SQL based) for consumption while enabling more modern scenarios around data science and machine learning that were originally not possible in the on-premises implementation of a data warehouse. This is primarily accomplished with a data lake, which serves as a no-silos data store supporting advanced data science and machine learning scenarios with cloud native services while retaining the familiar data warehouse, such as an SQL-based interface for BI users. In addition, the data administrators can isolate access of the data to the data warehouse for the BI teams using the familiar access control methods of the data warehouse. The applications running on premises can also be ported to the cloud over time to completely eliminate the need to maintain two sets of infrastructures. Further, the business can lower its costs overall by backing up the operational data into a data lake for a longer time period.

There are also a few challenges with this approach. The data engineers and administrators still need to maintain two sets of infrastructures: a data lake and a data warehouse. The flexibility of storing all kinds of data in a data lake also poses a challenge. Managing data in the data lake and assuming guarantees of data quality are huge challenges that data engineers and data administrators now have to solve—problems they did not have before. The data lake also runs the risk of growing into a data swamp if the data is not managed properly, hiding insights like a needle in a haystack. If BI users or business decision makers need new datasets, they must rely on the data engineers to process this data and load it into the warehouse, introducing a critical path. Further, if there is an interesting slice of data in the warehouse that the data scientists want to include for exploratory analysis, they need to load it back into the data lake, in a different data format as well as a different data store, increasing the complexity of sharing.

Data Lakehouse Architecture

Data lakehouse, a term popularized by Databricks (*https://oreil.ly/QKOFk*), is probably the biggest buzzword in the industry. According to a blog post (*https://oreil.ly/tirbC*) by Malav Parekh, a research analyst with 451 Research, Amazon first used the term *lake house*, with a space between "lake" and "house," when it released Redshift Spectrum (*https://oreil.ly/w-jLa*). The term gained momentum in the industry in January 2020 when a Databricks blog post (*https://oreil.ly/mDtEN*) called the data lakehouse a *new, open architecture* that combines the best elements of data lakes and data warehouses.

I distinctly remember the keynote at the Data and AI Summit (*https://oreil.ly/vccdT*) in 2020 where Ali Ghodsi announced the data lakehouse as a new paradigm and also introduced Delta Lake. There were multiple sessions on Delta Lake, with lines to get into them curving along the corridors of the conference hall. The growing popularity and ecosystem of the data lakehouse architecture support this claim of a new paradigm.

Data lakehouse architecture can be simply explained as a single platform that combines two functionalities:

- Data lake for analytics processing, data science, and machine learning scenarios
- Data warehouse for SQL interactive queries and BI scenarios

In other words, it refers to the ability to run SQL and BI scenarios on a data lake. This is a very attractive proposition for three reasons:

- Data lakes are much cheaper than data warehouses, making the lakehouse more cost-effective.
- No data movement or data copy is required to move data from the data lake to the data warehouse.
- Datasets can be freely shared between data scientists and BI teams by eliminating the bifurcated experiences and platforms.

Reference Architecture for the Data Lakehouse

A simplified representation of the data lakehouse architecture is provided in Figure 2-10. Note that you now run *all scenarios*—BI as well as data science—on a single platform, and you don't have a cloud data warehouse.

Well, if we had the option to run our BI scenarios on the data lake already, why didn't we do this in the first place? The simple answer is because data lakes by themselves are not really structured to support BI queries, and there are various technologies that have made the lakehouse a reality. Remember that data warehouses rely on highly structured data for faster query processing and supporting complex queries involving joins and aggregates, whereas data lakes are highly scalable object storage services, which store and transact on data, making no assumptions on the structure.

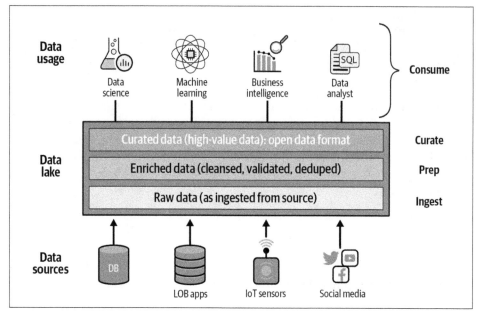

Figure 2-10. Data lakehouse architecture

Let's look at this in closer detail. Data warehouses offer the following advantages:

Schema definition and enforcement

> *Schema* is essentially the definition of the structure and type of data in your database. Data warehouses operate on highly structured data, which by definition means that you need to define and enforce this structure right at the point when you write the data. This is also called *schema on write*. For example, you can define that the age field in a table needs to be an integer, and if you attempt to write a noninteger value, there will be an error.

ACID-compliant transactions

> Data warehouses ensure that the transactions are ACID compliant, a quality that is critical to guarantee the integrity of high-value data typically stored in a warehouse. This integrity is very important because this data powers queries and dashboards used for critical operations that affect the revenue and operations of the company. For example, sales projections dashboards set revenue targets for the organization. ACID refers to four key properties of a transaction:

> *Atomicity*

>> Ensures that when a transaction is completed, there is a guarantee of integrity that the whole transaction was successful as a unit. For example, if you request the details of a customer in your query and ask for name, age,

location, and earning potential, you get all the details, not just the age and location alone.

Consistency
Ensures that all the appropriate data validation rules are followed, and only data that is permitted is written. If the validation is not successful, the database is rolled back to its previous state before the transaction. For example, if you want to add a new customer record to the database, and you have the right name and age but an invalid location, the whole transaction fails.

Isolation
Ensures that when concurrent transactions are processed, one does not affect the other. For example, if two users try to add the same customer to the database, the first one succeeds, and the second user gets an error since the customer is already present.

Durability
Ensures that after a successful transaction, there is a guarantee that the data is available. For example, when you successfully add customers to a database, even when there is a power failure or hardware outage, you can be assured that the customer data is intact.

Optimized for SQL
Most of the BI and data analyst tooling and ecosystem are optimized around SQL, and data warehouses offer a query engine that is optimized for SQL supporting these scenarios.

Data lakes offer the following advantages:

Ability to store and process unstructured data
Most of the emerging scenarios around advanced analytics, data science, and machine learning rely on processing unstructured data. Data lakes make no assumptions about the structure or schema of the data. When reading data from a data lake, you define a schema at the time of the read.

Low cost
Data lakes are highly optimized storage systems that offer a low cost of ownership to the user and let you store any amount of data you want without worrying about the rising expenses.

Rich data management
Data lakes offer a slew of capabilities to help manage the data, as we saw in the earlier sections. These include tiered storage, data replication, and data sharing capabilities.

Although unifying the data lake and the data warehouse into one architecture is attractive, the advantages of data lakes are the shortcomings of the data warehouse, and vice versa, and this has been hindering the lakehouse architecture for a long time.

However, with the growing adoption of data lakes across organizations and the proliferation of scenarios running on top of the data lakes, there has been a healthy growth of mindshare contributing to key technologies that make the data lakehouse paradigm a reality today. Some of these technologies include Delta Lake (*https://delta.io*), which originated in Databricks; Apache Iceberg (*https://iceberg.apache.org*), which originated in Netflix; and Apache Hudi (*https://hudi.apache.org*), which originated in Uber.

Although these technologies themselves are different and come at the problem from different perspectives, they have one thing in common: they have *defined the data* that gets stored in the data lake. This data format lays the foundation for providing the guarantees of the data warehouse (ACID-ish compliance, metadata handling, schema enforcement and evolution) on the data lake.

They accomplish this with three key components:

- Open file formats
- A metadata layer that defines the data
- Compute engines that understand these file formats and metadata layers

With these components, they take unstructured data stored as objects or files in a data lake and provide a new logical shape to them as a table. A *table* refers to data that is organized in logical rows and columns, as shown in Figure 2-11.

> To enable a data lakehouse architecture, you need to ensure that you leverage one of the open data technologies, such as Apache Iceberg, Delta Lake, or Apache Hudi, as well as a compute framework that understands and respects these formats. Cloud providers are continuing to work on tool sets and services that simplify the architecture and operationalization of the data lakehouse. An example worth calling out is AWS services that make a data lakehouse implementation easier (*https://oreil.ly/oVDbT*) by leveraging AWS Glue (*https://aws.amazon.com/glue*) for data integration and orchestration, Amazon S3 (*https://aws.amazon.com/s3*) as the cloud data lake storage, and Amazon Athena (*https://aws.amazon.com/athena*) to query data from S3 using standard SQL that is familiar to BI users.

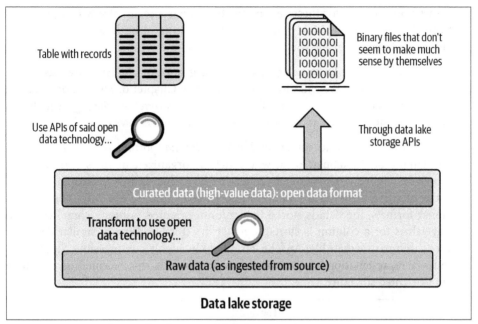

Figure 2-11. Open data technologies and lakehouse architecture

Data formats

We have already established that the data format is crucial to the data lakehouse architecture, but why is that the case? As we saw earlier, data in a data warehouse has strong guarantees around integrity; to enable similar guarantees for the data in a data lake, it is important to keep the data bound to a few key rules. As an analogy, a child needs to play by certain rules in a classroom to create an environment that is conducive to learning, but the same child can run amok and explore at will at a park. Think of what you would need to do if you were to set up a classroom in a park; the open data formats attempt to ensure that the data is bounded by certain rules in an unstructured environment, which, in this case, is the data lake storage.

The data format is key to a lakehouse architecture for the following reasons:

- The data stored needs to *adhere to a schema*, which is defined by the metadata (data that describes that tabular structure of the dataset). *Schema* here refers to a defined representation or description of the data.

- The data stored is *optimized for queries*, especially to support the BI use cases that largely use SQL-like queries. This optimization is crucial to support query performance that is comparable to a data warehouse.

As it turns out, solving for these requirements also has a really nice benefit, which is that this data tends to be highly compressible, resulting in both faster performance and lower cost, which means you could have your cake and eat it too.

Specialized formats like Delta Lake, Apache Iceberg, and Apache Hudi are used in the data lake architectures. We will discuss them more in Chapter 6. They all derive from a fundamental data format, Apache Parquet (*https://parquet.apache.org*), which is a columnar data storage format used by the Apache Hadoop ecosystem.

Let's do a small detour to understand what *columnar format* means. Remember, we are talking about tabular data, where data is organized in rows and columns, as shown in Figure 2-12. When it comes to how this data is stored in the data lake, the intuitive thinking is you store one record—that is, one row—together. In columnar formats, the data is stored in a column-oriented fashion, where data with similar values for a column is stored together. It's this bundling of similar data that enables columnar formats like Apache Parquet to be highly compressible. Figure 2-12 provides a representation of the same data stored in a row-oriented as well as a column-oriented structure.

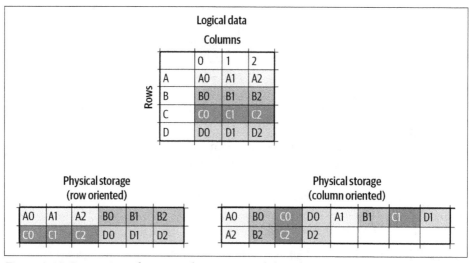

Figure 2-12. Row-oriented versus column-oriented data formats

We will address Apache Parquet in more detail in Chapter 4. Open data technologies use Apache Parquet as their underlying data format so that they can leverage the optimizations for Apache Parquet to optimize for queries.

Metadata

Metadata simply refers to data about the data. For example, if you have a table with 1,000 rows stored as chunks of 100 rows in each dataset, metadata is associated with each chunk that describes the data stored, such as this chunk has rows 101–200, containing values in the last name column starting with A–B. In addition, there is metadata stored at the table level that has pointers to the different chunks.

This metadata is not very relevant for the end user but is very relevant to compute engines that operate on data. These compute engines read the metadata and then go fetch the relevant data. Technologies like Apache Iceberg, Delta Lake, and Apache Hudi have their own versions of metadata to determine how data is stored and organized across the different Parquet files, what data is getting updated, and when so that they can offer data integrity and consistency and handshake with the compute engines to optimize for specific scenarios.

While all are suitable options, each was designed with a specific purpose in mind, and you'll want to consider this as you design your architecture. Delta Lake by Databricks is optimized for running highly performant SQL queries on the data lake, leveraging the metadata to do intelligent data skipping to read only the data required to serve the queries. Apache Hudi was made open source by Uber and was primarily designed to support incremental updates as well as fast query performance with columnar formats. Apache Iceberg was made open source by Netflix, primarily to support refreshing datasets (e.g., support updates to existing data on an append-only storage system like S3) in addition to reads by a plethora of compute engines, such as Apache Spark, Trino (Presto SQL), Apache Hive, and Apache Flink to varying degrees.

Compute engines

Unlike with the data warehouses where compute and storage are optimized and offered together as one service, running a data lakehouse requires using the right compute engines to leverage the optimizations offered by the data formats and metadata that are used to optimize the data storage. In other words, data is optimized to be written as a table in storage, and you need a compute engine to understand and read the table for effectively querying the data.

For example, in the case of Delta Lake, a format developed by Databricks, the compute component—that is, their Spark engine—is optimized for operating on Delta tables and further enhances performance with caching for faster performance and a Bloom filter index for effective data skipping. We will discuss the engines in deeper detail in Chapter 6.

Sample Use Case for Data Lakehouse Architecture

Klodars Corporation will leverage the data lake by loading data from its operational data bases into the data lake storage, similar to what we saw in the modern data warehouse architecture. Let's take a closer look at how this architecture affects the business.

The data engineering team will now use tools like Apache Spark to process the structured data from its database dump and from the website clickstream to generate high-value data that shows the shopping and sales trends over time. The team will also process the social media feeds and extract data that pertains to rain and winter gear as well as any associated purchases the same feeds indicate.

Let's now move on to how this extracted data will be processed. The data engineering team will generate high-value data on a scheduled basis (e.g., daily) on sales trends, inventory and supply, website-browsing trends, and social media trends around rain and winter gear. Now, instead of loading data into the warehouse, the business analysts can start querying this data using their familiar tool of choice based on SQL, as well as modern querying tools like Presto, without having to move the data. Similar to the modern data warehouse pattern, the data scientists can bring their own datasets, such as the weather data, as well as explore data that is already in the data lake.

The lakehouse provides a key advantage over the modern data warehouse by eliminating the need to have two places to store the same data. Let's say that the data science team leveraged its new datasets, such as the weather data, and built a new dataset that correlates sales with the weather. The business analysts have this data ready to go for their deeper analysis since everyone is using the same data store, and possibly the same data formats. Similarly, if the business analysis generated a specific filtered dataset, the data scientists can start using this for their analysis.

Take a moment to think about what this means and what the impact is. This completely explodes the scenarios, promoting the cross-pollination of insights between the different classes of consumers of the data platform. A shared platform with no silos implies that the data generated by the BI analysts and the data scientists is available for both to further innovate on, thereby increasing the value of data multifold for Klodars Corporation. A representation of the data lakehouse architecture at Klodars Corporation is presented in Figure 2-13.

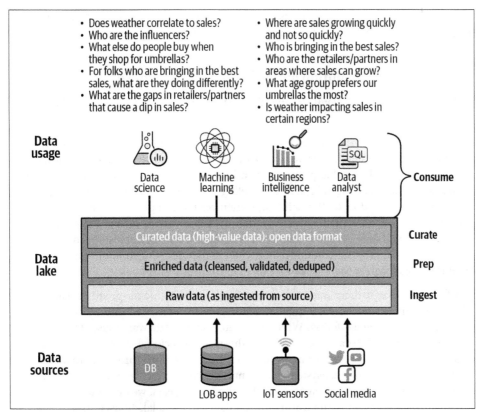

Figure 2-13. How Klodars Corporation leverages the data lakehouse architecture

Benefits and Challenges of the Data Lakehouse Architecture

Data lakehouses offer the key benefit of being able to run performant BI/SQL-based scenarios directly on the data lake, right alongside the other exploratory data science and machine learning scenarios. As we saw in the use case, this also promotes sharing across the various segments of users of the data platform, giving rise to new scenarios. Further, data lakes end up being very cost-effective when compared to data warehouses.

Having said that, there is certainly a challenge as well. As we saw in the architecture sections, constructing a data lakehouse requires careful design and architecture assembling the right data format and the compute engine to achieve the most optimized solution, resulting in faster performance. Without proper planning, many things could go awry, which we'll discuss in detail in Chapter 4. Data warehouses offer this optimized path right out of the box; however, they are not truly open. While I have no crystal ball, given the rapid pace of development in the data lakehouse architecture, my bet is that this is an area that is going to see quick innovations, resulting in a simplified end-to-end experience in the coming years.

Evolution of the Cloud Data Lakehouse

With Tomer Shiran, cofounder and CPO of Dremio Corporation (https://www.dre mio.com)

Evolution to a cloud data lakehouse architecture is in a lot of ways very similar to the evolution from a client server to a microservices architecture for cloud applications. There is a very clear value proposition in breaking the silos between data lake and data warehouse. Having said that, the tooling ecosystem and the barriers to getting started are high, due to the skills and engineering complexities. Very much like microservices, the data lakehouse is seeing rapid innovations in this space, such that this barrier will only get lower and lower with time. I had an interesting conversation with Tomer Shiran, the cofounder and CPO of Dremio Corporation, on this exact topic and had a great set of takeaways that I'm sharing in this book.

A few decades ago, there was an evolution from a monolithic on-premises data ware-house architecture where compute and storage were colocated into a disaggregated compute and storage offering. While this enables cloud data warehouses to efficiently scale compute and storage independently, this was still a closed system. This disaggregation solved a pain point for many and laid the foundations for the cloud data lake, which enabled an open ecosystem where multiple compute engines could transact on the same data, as shown in Figure 2-14. For the last 50 years, we brought data into the compute engine. Now, in the world of cloud data lakes and lakehouses, data is its own tier as a first-class entity in the architecture, and the engines come to the data instead of the other way around. This shift introduced the notion of building a solution with components from different vendors, avoiding a lock-in situation where only one vendor could be used. The reason data lake has a market cap in the hundreds of millions of dollars today is because of the cloud. The cloud enabled the ability to rely on an infrastructure that is available in all regions and can elastically scale, making data ubiquitous and a key growth driver that organizations now heavily rely on.

The open data formats are enabling an open data architecture while maintaining the integrity of the data as an asset, which was not originally possible because of the shortcomings of cloud object storage. The open data formats also fostered open source technologies that rallied a community around these formats to collaboratively improve these offerings. Cloud data lakehouse is essentially cloud data warehouse 2.0.

Anytime there is a transition in architecture, it starts off as difficult and then gets eas-ier over time. This was the case when we moved from mainframes to a client/server architecture, and then to microservices. When there is a clear value proposition, the industry gets better at building tooling around it, which makes it easier for everyone to adopt. Originally, cloud data lakehouses were only used in tech companies that were on the cutting edge. Now that companies have come along to simplify the data lakehouse architecture, enterprises are adopting the cloud data lakehouse. Although these enterprises are not on the bleeding edge of technology, they are big enough to have teams working on the right problems. We are also beginning to see data lakehouses be adopted by smaller motivated firms that have a couple of data analysts and data engineers. The barrier to getting started is lowered every day, and the vision is to make it as easy to use as a database service.

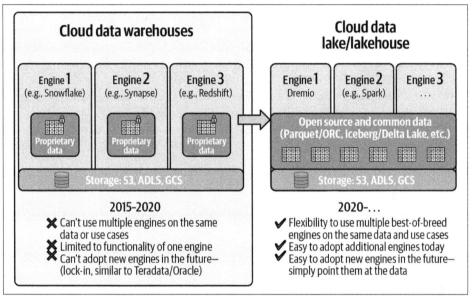

Figure 2-14. Evolution from cloud data warehouses to cloud data lakehouses (courtesy of Tomer Shiran)

Data Warehouses and Unstructured Data

If data lakes can start supporting data warehouse scenarios, can data warehouses start supporting data lake scenarios as well? The answer is a surprising yes. As we saw in the previous section, Azure Synapse Analytics offers a unified data platform for Spark, machine learning, and SQL. Google BigQuery supports storing unstructured data and offers Parquet support natively; it also supports querying data stored in GCS. Snowflake has recently launched support for unstructured data (*https://oreil.ly/bfI-Y*) as well. Whether data lakes are supporting data warehouses or vice versa, our current innovations clearly indicate that the need for a unified data platform and a data platform without silos is the way forward.

Data Mesh

In 2019, Zhamak Dehghani, Director of Emerging Technologies at Thoughtworks, wrote an article on data mesh (*https://oreil.ly/sIr1J*) that laid the foundations for the *data mesh architecture*, which enables an organization to run the data infrastructure and operations in a decentralized fashion, thereby democratizing data and insights across the organization. Let's take a look at why this decentralized data mesh is important or relevant.

So far, we have talked about data lakes as a central repository of data and intelligence for an organization and the technology choices. The way this has manifested in architectures is as a centrally managed infrastructure. Now let's take a look at who in the organization is responsible for designing and operationalizing the data lake. The data extraction and processing are administered by a central team, typically referred to as the data platform team, data infrastructure team, data engineering team, or <insert your favorite variation here>. For the purposes of this section, we'll refer to this team as the *data platform team*.

The data platform team typically owns the following roles:

Data platform architecture
Designs the infrastructure for the compute and storage components that serve the needs of the organization.

Data management
Organizes the datasets on the cloud; applies data management policies to ensure the data meets the compliance needs of the organization around data retention and data residency.

Data governance
Controls who has access to what data, provides a catalog so consumers of the data platform can discover the datasets, and manages audits.

Data ingestion
Typically owns the ingestion of data from various sources, on-premises systems, IoT, and so on, as well as potentially the data preparation, so it's ready to be consumed. In some cases, the data platform team tends to delegate this ingestion to the consumers of the data lake.

In other words, the data infrastructure was a monolithic unit managed by a central team while the rest of the organization focused on the consumption scenarios: BI, data science, or other needs. As the number of scenarios based on data grows, and the organization increases, this data platform team, which is typically a lean organization, can easily be buried with requests from across the organization, and they end up on the critical path for data, introducing a bottleneck.

Data mesh architecture calls for a culture shift to viewing data as a product that can be shared across organizations, as opposed to data as an asset/entity that needs to be collected and processed.

What does this culture shift mean? At this point, I would like to quote a great set of principles that Zhamak Dehghani calls out in her book *Data Mesh* (*https://oreil.ly/ F0Eop*) (O'Reilly):

- *Organizationally*, there is a shift in responsibility from a central data platform organization that does everything to a decentralized model where there are specialists in every business domain focusing on data needs.
- *Architecturally*, there is a shift from a monolithic implementation of a large central data warehouse or a data lake to a distributed mesh of data lakes and data warehouses that still make a single logical representation of data by sharing insights and data between them.
- *Technologically*, there is a shift from thinking about data as a separate entity and platform to integrated solutions that treat data and business code as a unit together.
- *Operationally*, there is a shift from a top-down directive from a central operational model on data governance to a federated model where every business domain owns and respects the policies of the organization.
- *Principally*, there is a shift from data treated as an asset that is collected to a product that serves and delights its users.

Reference Architecture

Data mesh relies on a distributed architecture that consists of domains. Each domain is an independent unit of data and its associated storage and compute components. When an organization contains various product units, each with its own data needs, each product team owns a domain that is operated and governed independently by the product team. The roles and responsibilities include the following:

- The central data platform team formulates and maintains a set of blueprints/reference patterns on the architecture of the compute, storage, and data components.
- The product teams implement these blueprints to operationalize their domains.

This allows the product teams/domains to use the infrastructure or technology of their choice; for example, one unit could use a lakehouse architecture on AWS, and another unit could implement a modern data warehouse architecture on Microsoft Azure while still sharing the data and insights between them. The key principle here is that the data in the domains is shared across the organization within the compliance and governance boundaries to adhere to the principles of a no-silo logical data lake that still promotes sharing of data and insights. A representation of a data mesh architecture is presented in Figure 2-15.

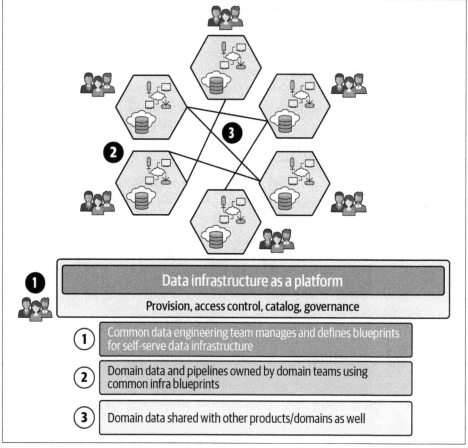

Figure 2-15. Data mesh architecture

Sample Use Case for a Data Mesh Architecture

Klodars Corporation was running fine as long as its software products and teams were smaller. However, as the business grew and launched in more regions, the teams and organization grew significantly, and the central data platform was no longer able to scale to the needs. Further, as Klodars Corporation acquired other companies on different technology stacks, it was hard for them to integrate as one unit. Alice and her team on the central data platform decided to implement a data mesh architecture.

The central data platform team at Klodars Corporation publishes the architecture, along with deployment and configuration scripts to automate the domain setup, and they set up data governance, compliance, and the data sharing infrastructure. Klodars Corporation has sales, marketing, and customer success teams that implement their domains and share their insights with other organizations. The sales team finds that the modern data warehouse architecture suits its needs, given that it has a prolific usage of operational databases, and the customer success team finds the lakehouse architecture better for its needs, given the diversity of data sources that can benefit both its BI and data science teams. The data mesh pattern enables Klodars Corporation to give this freedom of choice to its domains while promoting the sharing of data, maintaining the proposition of a unified data platform. Further, the companies that Klodars Corporation acquired were able to retain their existing data lakes with minor tweaks. When Klodars Corporation wants to expand to winter gear, it can effectively share its insights with the ski corporations it partners with to promote a better partnership, extending the data mesh architecture. Klodars Corporation is growing rapidly and wants to expand its business to Europe, which has unique data residency and other compliance requirements. It can set up domains specific to the European Union (EU) that also respect EU-specific requirements without incurring a huge development or rearchitecture effort. Further down the road, when Klodars Corporation acquires other companies, it can onboard the data platforms of the companies they acquired as domains to its existing data mesh. A representation of the data mesh architecture at Klodars Corporation is depicted in Figure 2-16.

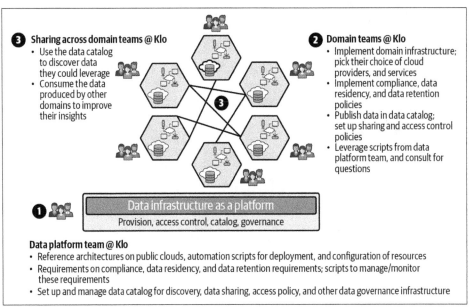

Figure 2-16. How Klodars Corporation leverages the data mesh architecture

Challenges and Benefits of a Data Mesh Architecture

Data mesh has a unique value proposition, not just offering scale of infrastructure and scenarios but also helping shift the organization's culture around data, as we saw in the previous section. Data mesh architecture offers the following benefits, as the use case showed:

- Enables a self-serve architecture that is extensible to the growth of the organization and the diversity of data

- Offers the flexibility of choice of architecture and platforms to the domains

- Promotes data as a culture across the organization and not as the role of a small team, avoiding bottlenecks

There are certainly challenges with this approach as well. First and foremost, this relies on individual product teams having skilled software developers available, which is not always the case. Next, a data lake architecture comes with its own complexities from the diversity of the data and the ecosystem; adding a distributed layer increases this complexity. Having said that, investing in this up front sets an organization up for success, and based on growing popularity of the data mesh, I would make an educated guess that there is going to be rapid innovation in simplifying the deployment and management of this architecture as well.

What Is the Right Architecture for Me?

We talked about three key popular cloud data lake architectures in this section:

- Modern data warehouse architecture, which is commonly prevalent in organizations

- Data lakehouse architecture, which enables BI scenarios to run on the data lake directly

- Data mesh architecture, which offers a decentralized approach to managing and operating the cloud data lake

How do you know which architecture to pick? And how do you know you are right? While we all learn as we go, there are a set of fundamental principles we can apply to help you move in the right direction.

Know Your Customers

As with every project, start defining the goals that you know you have to meet in a prioritized order as well as your customer segments. You can start with one or more of the following customer segments, depending on what your organization needs:

BI/data analysts
> Prepare datasets for them to analyze using the data lake. This can be done by running scheduled jobs that ingest data from various sources, and data processing to generate datasets for your BI users.

Data scientists/exploratory analysis
> Set up an infrastructure to which data scientists can bring their own datasets for analysis. You can optionally manage the ingest from known sources and make datasets available to them on the data lake.

I have known customers who started their data lake journey for data scientists while they continued to run their data warehouses; they have no technical debt or existing compatibility and start fresh with their data lake to support the first set of scenarios for the organization. I have also known customers who have started their data lake journey by solving the needs for their BI users on the lake; in this case, their goals are to modernize their data infrastructure to support new scenarios while maintaining support for their existing pipelines, so they have some allowances to rearchitect, while the priority is to keep the lights on. I have also seen some customers use the data lake as a failover plan while they continued to run their on-premises systems, in which case, their cloud architecture had to be a replica of their on-premises systems, and they will think about modernization in a later phase. You could fit into one of these buckets or have your own scenarios. Ultimately, knowing your customers is the first step: talk to your customers and your business decision makers, understand the role of data in your organization today, and show them the potential.

Know Your Business Drivers

While new technology is utterly fascinating, and the reason I continue doing whatever I do, we always need to remember that technology is a means to the end, and every decision needs to be grounded in a problem you are trying to solve for your organization. There are many business drivers that lead organizations to a cloud data lake. Let's take a look at a few of them:

Cost
> Moving to a cloud data lake guarantees a reduction in your TCO, and in my experience, this remains one of the top drivers for organizations to move to the cloud data lake approach. Make sure to triangulate your decisions on architecture with the goal of how much cost reduction this would offer.

New scenarios
> Although some organizations have an existing data infrastructure, they are motivated to move to the cloud data lake to leverage the growing ecosystem of modern technologies, such as machine learning or real-time analytics, to differentiate their business and their product. If this is your motivation, you are leaning toward delivering value with these new scenarios and should define

the goals appropriately. Are you going to increase adoption with new marketing campaigns or deliver value with intelligent products? Again, measure your technology choices against these goals.

Time

While an organization's move to the cloud can be motivated by costs, modern scenarios, and other drivers, time sometimes dictates the technology and architecture choices. I have seen customers set a road map to move to the cloud while support runs out on their on-premises hardware or software licenses. Then your technology/architecture choices are dictated by the time available.

Consider Your Growth and Future Scenarios

While your customer requirements and business drivers define the prioritization of your technology and architecture decisions, you need to ensure that the design you pick does not paint you into a corner. For example, if your data lake infrastructure is motivated by requirements from the marketing department, which needs to run personalized campaigns and understand your customer segments better, you will design the first version of your data lake architecture to meet these needs—ensure that you focus on ingesting data from your customer systems and from social media feeds, and generate datasets that can be used by business analysts to pick the high-priority segments they want to customize their campaigns for. However, your design should anticipate more scenarios and more customers when this first scenario is successful. I have worked with customers who always assumed that the data engineering team would be the sole team with access to data in the data lake and did not implement the right set of security and access controls, only to find the scenarios growing rapidly, with everyone having access to everything and causing accidental data deletes. So even if you have one customer, think about how you would design a system with a multitude of users, focusing on data organization, security, and governance. We will look at these in detail in Chapter 3.

Design Considerations

When I talk to customers about their data lake solution, I'm often asked to recommend the cheapest approach or the fastest approach, and my answer is always "It depends," which I give with a smile. Given the flexibility and the diversity of the cloud data lake solutions and the ecosystem of software and platforms, selecting the right fit and the right approach is almost like planning the budget to run your house. While we could make blanket statements like "Costco has great prices!" the less understood subtext is "and it relies on you to ensure that you don't waste the items you buy in bulk." Cloud data lakes offer flexibility and lower cost, but they rely on the data platform team to ensure they run in an optimized fashion. In Table 2-1, I have attempted to provide an assessment of these architectures against a few predictable dimensions, so you can use it as a starting point to determine the right fit for you.

Table 2-1. Comparison of architectures

Architecture	Total cost of solution	Flexibility of scenarios	Complexity of development	Maturity of ecosystem	Organizational maturity required
Cloud data warehouse	**High:** given that cloud data warehouses rely on proprietary data formats and offer an end-to-end solution, the cost is high.	**Low:** cloud data warehouses are optimized for BI/SQL-based scenarios; there is some support for data science/exploratory scenarios, which is restrictive due to format constraints.	**Low:** there are fewer moving parts, and you can get started almost immediately with an end-to-end solution.	**High** for SQL/BI scenarios. **Low** for other scenarios.	**Low:** the tools and ecosystem are largely well understood and ready to be consumed by organizations of any shape/size.
Modern data warehouse	**Medium:** the data preparation and historical data can be moved to the data lake at a lower cost; you still need a cloud warehouse, which is expensive.	**Medium:** a diverse ecosystem of tools and more exploratory scenarios are supported in the data lake; correlating data in the warehouse and data lake needs data copies.	**Medium:** the data engineering team needs to ensure that the data lake design is efficient and scalable; plenty of guidance and considerations are available, including this book.	**Medium:** the data preparation and data engineering ecosystem, such as Spark/Hadoop, has a higher maturity; tuning for performance and scale is needed. **High** for consumption via data warehouse.	**Medium:** the data platform team needs to be skilled up to understand the needs of the organization and make the right design choices to support those needs.
Data lakehouse	**Low:** the data lake storage acts as the unified repository with no data movement required; compute engines are largely stateless and can be spun up and down on demand.	**High:** the flexibility of running more scenarios with a diverse ecosystem enables more exploratory analysis, such as data science, and ease of sharing of data between BI and data science teams.	**Medium to High:** careful choice of the right datasets and the open data format is needed to support the lakehouse architecture.	**Medium to High:** while technologies like Delta Lake, Apache Iceberg, and Apache Hudi are gaining maturity and adoption, this architecture requires thoughtful design today.	**Medium to High:** the data platform team needs to be skilled up to understand the needs of the organization and the technology choices that are still new.
Data mesh	**Medium:** while the distributed design ensures the cost is lower, a lot of investment is required in automation, blueprint, and data governance solutions	**High:** there is flexibility in supporting different architectures and solutions in the same organization, and there are no bottlenecks on a central lean organization.	**High:** this relies on an end-to-end automated solution and an architecture that scales to 10X growth and sharing across architectures/cloud solutions.	**Low:** relatively nascent in guidance and available tool sets.	**High:** the data platform and product/domain teams need to be skilled up in data lakes.

Let's look at this data in another way. Figure 2-17 shows a trade-off between cost and complexity across the different architectures.

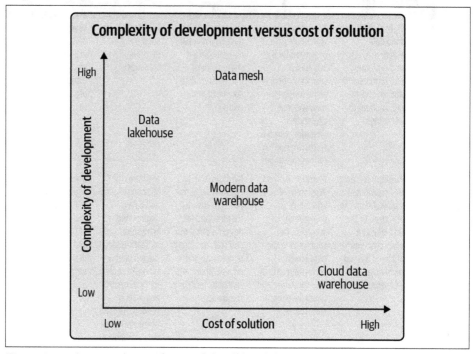

Figure 2-17. Cost versus complexity of cloud data lake architectures

Hybrid Approaches

Depending on your organizational needs, the maturity of your scenarios, and your data platform strategy, you could end up having a hybrid approach to your data lake. As an example, although most of the organization runs on a cloud data warehouse as its central data repository, there is a center of innovation working with a set of handpicked scenarios on a data lake architecture, which is gradually expanded to the rest of the company. Or, while most of the organization adopts a data lakehouse architecture, some teams still depend on legacy infrastructure that would take years to move.

The nuances of your scenarios may be so niche or specific to your organization that they are out of the scope of this book. However, the principles that we discussed in this chapter will help you ask the right questions and make an informed choice about the data lake architecture.

The big data ecosystem and cloud data lake architecture is a field of rapid innovation. I'm pretty sure that by the time I finish this chapter, the needle will have already been moved on something.

Summary

In this chapter, we took a deeper look at three key architectures for the cloud data lake, and we saw how they compare with the traditional cloud data warehouse architecture. First, we went over the modern data warehouse architecture, where you collect and process data in a data lake to transform your raw data with relatively lower-value density into high-value structured data and load the high-value data into a cloud data warehouse for supporting BI scenarios. Next, we built on this with the data lakehouse architecture, which supports BI scenarios (in addition to data engineering and data science scenarios) directly on the data lake, eliminating the need for a cloud data warehouse. Then, we explored the data mesh architecture, which offers a decentralized approach to managing and operating the data lake, enabling a sustainable way to scale to the growing needs and rapid proliferation of data across the organization. Finally, we put all of these in perspective together with factors like the maturity, skill sets, and size of your organization to help you formulate the right cloud data lake architecture for your organization. In Chapter 3, we will focus more on the "data" part of the cloud data lake: considerations for organizing, managing, securing, and governing the data in your data lake.

Design Considerations for Your Data Lake

Have no fear of perfection—you will never reach it.

—Salvador Dali

In Chapters 1 and 2, we got a 10,000-foot view of what cloud data lakes are and some widely used data lake architectures on the cloud. The information in the first two chapters gives you enough context to start architecting your cloud data lake design; you must be able to at least take a dry-erase marker and sketch a block diagram that represents the components of your cloud data lake architecture and how they interact.

In this chapter, we are going to dive into the details of the implementation of the cloud data lake architecture. As you will recall, the cloud data lake architecture consists of a diverse set of IaaS, PaaS, and SaaS products that are assembled into an end-to-end solution. Think of these individual services as Lego blocks and your solution as the structure you build with Lego pieces. You might end up building a fort or a dragon or a spaceship—the choices are limited only by your creativity (and business needs). However, there are a few basics you need to understand, which is what we are looking at in this chapter.

We will continue to use Klodars Corporation to illustrate some examples of the decision choices.

Setting Up the Cloud Data Lake Infrastructure

Most cloud data lake architectures fall under one of two categories:

- You want to build your cloud data lake from scratch on the cloud. You don't have a prior data lake or data warehouse implementation and are starting from a clean slate.

- You want to migrate your data lake from either your on-premises systems or other cloud providers to the cloud. In this case, you already have an existing implementation, either as a data warehouse or a data lake, that you will move to the cloud.

Your first steps on your journey to the cloud largely remain the same in either case. You will choose the cloud provider, you will choose the services, and you will set up your infrastructure. The cloud encompasses a wide variety of offerings that are available for you to choose from, each having its strengths and opportunities, so before you move to the cloud, the first thing to remember is that there is no silver bullet or prescribed 12-step process when it comes to making this transition. However, having worked with many customers as well as on cloud migrations myself, I have condensed the customer journey into a decision framework, which consists of the following key steps, as illustrated in Figure 3-1:

1. Identify your goals.

2. Plan your architecture and deliverables.

3. Implement the cloud data lake, either from scratch or by migrating your existing system to the cloud.

4. Operationalize and release.

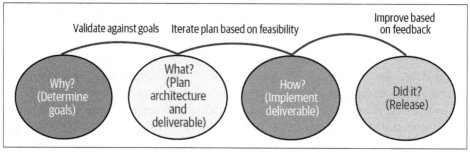

Figure 3-1. Framework to plan your cloud data lake implementation

Let's take a closer look at each of these steps in practice.

Identify Your Goals

As we saw in Chapter 1, data lakes are critical to unlocking key insights to inform and transform the business. However, with the myriad possibilities, it's very important to identify the specific goals that data would provide for your organization. These goals help you decide what kind of data and processing you need to prioritize for your business.

As a first step, you need to determine who the customers of your data lake are; they can either be departments within your organization (e.g., HR, finance, supply chain) or customers external to your organization (e.g., customers who consume your dashboards). Additionally, look at the problems with your own data lake implementation, if any. For example, your current problems could be related to the high cost of datacenters and operations eating into your budget, or to your current hardware running out of support, or even to your current architecture not being able to serve advanced scenarios around data science and machine learning, which is making your business lose advantage in a competitive market. Once you talk to your various customers and inventory their top-of-mind problems, you can identify the subset of the top problems where data can help. Your goal for the data lake implementation will be to solve these problems, as illustrated in Figure 3-2.

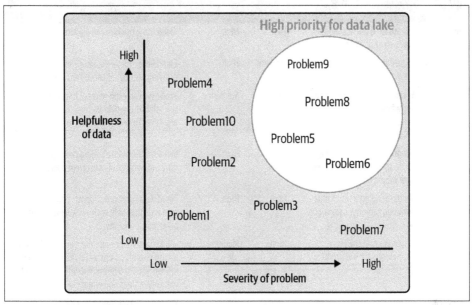

Figure 3-2. Define goals of your data lake

As shown in Figure 3-2, your team has identified 10 problems by talking to your various consumers. However, when you plot then on a graph of high severity versus how useful a cloud data lake could be in solving these problems, you can see that you should prioritize Problem5, Problem6, Problem8, and Problem9 because they rank high in severity as well as in the usefulness of a cloud data lake.

How Klodars Corporation defined the data lake goals

As we saw in Chapter 2, Klodars Corporation currently has legacy applications leveraging operational databases (SQL server) to manage its inventory and sales, and customer relationship management (CRM) software (such as Salesforce) to manage its customer profile and interactions. When Klodars Corporation hits growing pains as it rapidly expands across the state of Washington and neighboring states, along with the growth of its online business, its software development leader, Alice, pitches the idea of developing a data lake to her executives, and they are eager to invest in the approach.

The rubber has hit the road, and Alice begins planning the data lake implementation project. The very first step she takes is to inventory the problems across the organization, and she comes up with the list outlined in Table 3-1.

Table 3-1. Inventory of problems at Klodars Corporation along with relevance to data

Customer	Problem	Severity of problem	Helpfulness of data lake	How cloud data lake can help
Engineering	Database is not scaling to growth of business.	High	High	Cloud infrastructure can elastically scale.
Sales	Sales queries are painstakingly slow.	Medium	High	Cloud infrastructure scaling can support a growing number of concurrent users.
Sales	I can't prioritize which retailer or wholesale distributor to engage outside the state of Washington.	High	Medium	While we can explore retail datasets to identify the sales, this would be more experimental and takes time to mature.
Marketing	Queries are taking a really long time to run; complex queries are timing out.	High	High	Cloud infrastructure scaling can support a growing number of concurrent users.
Marketing	I am spending a lot of time running targeted campaigns.	High	High	Cloud data lakes can support data science scenarios that help with personalized and targeted campaigns.
Marketing	I need to find the right influencers for our product.	High	Medium	While data science and machine learning can identify insights from social media, the specific influencers are determined with more one-to-one connections and engagements.
Exec team	I need to understand what product offerings we can start expanding to beyond winter gear.	Medium	High	We can run data science models on retail datasets to understand the behavior of customers buying winter gear to come up with useful product recommendations.

Based on this inventory, Alice defined the goals of her data lake implementation as follows and reviews it with her stakeholders to finalize the goals:

- (*Must have*) Support better scale and performance for existing sales and marketing dashboards as measured by a 50% increase in query performance at the 75th percentile.

- (*Must have*) Support data science models on the data lake as measured by a pilot engagement on product offering recommendations to the executive team.

- (*Nice to have*) Support more data science models on the data lake as measured by the next set of scenarios on partnership identification for sales and by influencer recommendation for marketing.

Plan Your Architecture and Deliverables

Once the goals are defined for the data lake, the next step is to define the architecture and the deliverables. As we saw in Chapter 2, a variety of architecture patterns are commonly used, each with its design considerations, as described in "Design Considerations" on page 58. Consider the goals of your data lake along with other factors, such as the organizational maturity, to determine the right architecture for your data lake. Following are some of these common considerations for determining the architecture:

Cost of the solution
> Identify both the initial cost of setting up as well as the longer-term cost of maintaining your solution, and weigh them against the benefits. A data lake is much cheaper than a data warehouse; however, a data warehouse is easier to get up and running.

Time taken for the implementation
> In the world of software development, developer and operational time is as important as the dollar bills in terms of cost, so factor in the people and operational aspects into your calculations and get an estimate of the time and effort required for the solution. If you have existing hardware that is reaching end of life, you need to pick a pattern/architecture that can be implemented before the existing hardware runs out of support.

Backward compatibility
> When you have an existing data infrastructure you need to move to the cloud, it is reasonable to assume that your cloud migration will be done in phases. You need to ensure that while you are moving certain chunks of your solution to the cloud, you can guarantee business continuity without much disruption for your existing applications and consumers. If you have an existing operational database that is supporting dashboards, then ensuring there is compatibility for the existing applications is a consideration you need to factor in.

Organizational maturity

This is an often-ignored factor in most marketing materials. When you are talking to cloud providers or ISVs, make sure to discuss the current skill sets and data culture of your organization and understand how their solutions could serve the current state while you plan on upskilling your organization and transforming its culture. For example, an architecture optimized for data science is not a best fit if you haven't yet hired data scientists.

Once you decide on the architecture, you can collaborate with your customers and define the goals for your cloud data lake architecture based on the prioritized list of scenarios you will support. You can then create a project plan that tracks the timelines and deliverables, and overall progress towards your goals.

How Klodars Corporation planned their architecture and deliverables

Based on the goals defined for the cloud data lake implementation, Alice and her team then investigate different architecture choices using the following guiding principles:

- There is minimal/no disruption to the existing dashboards that sales and marketing teams consume.
- The dashboards need to scale to the growth of the data and address the performance issues faced by customers.
- The data science scenarios need to be addressed as part of the new platform. This includes product recommendations for the executive team, distributor/retailer recommendations to sales teams, and influencer recommendations to marketing teams.
- Given the criticality of the dashboards to the business and the projected future growth that needs to be factored in, the new architecture needs to be rolled out in the next six months.

They evaluate the following architecture patterns on the cloud (this is fairly agnostic of the specific provider):

Cloud data warehouse

In this architecture pattern, there is no cloud data lake involved, and the primary component would be a cloud data warehouse. If you would like a refresher on cloud data warehouses, refer to "Cloud Data Warehouses" on page 34. While this would take the least time to implement and be a seamless experience for the business analysts from sales and marketing teams, the data science capabilities are limited. As a result, this could serve as a pilot, but there might be roadblocks when the scenarios get more advanced, such as bringing in more diverse datasets.

Note that cloud data warehouses like Snowflake are blurring the boundaries between data warehouse and data lake. At the point when I'm writing this book, I would personally qualify Snowflake as a data warehouse, mainly because the primary use case for Snowflake is operating on structured data.

Modern data warehouse

As we saw in "Modern Data Warehouse Architecture" on page 36, this involves leveraging cloud data lake storage for the data collection and processing and a cloud data warehouse for BI scenarios. This would take a bit longer to implement than the cloud data warehouse. However, the rich set of data science capabilities on the data lake would help the team focus on the pilots while also supporting the data analysts through the data warehouse. Additionally, the data lake offers cheaper storage to preserve multiple snapshots of historical data of the on-premises databases.

Data lakehouse

As we saw in "Data Lakehouse Architecture" on page 40, this involves leveraging a cloud data lake storage for the end-to-end implementation without requiring a cloud data warehouse component. This is very attractive for the team given the support for both data science and data analyst scenarios; however, they soon realize that upskilling is required for the tooling support and automation end to end.

The team did not evaluate the data mesh architecture because it wanted to focus on maintaining central control of the end-to-end implementation. They will evaluate the data mesh during the next phase of the project.

The team settled on a modern data warehouse architecture, because it provided a smoother transition from the current architecture while offering support for data science. The team also plans to investigate data lakehouse and data mesh architectures in the next phase of the project once they are up and running on the cloud.

As shown in Figure 3-3, the modern data warehouse architecture for Klodars Corporation consists of the following components:

- A cloud data lake storage that acts as a central repository of the data
- Ingestion systems that upload data from existing sources, such as the operational data store, as well as new data sources, such as social media, into the cloud data lake
- Data processing engines that process data from the cloud data lake storage with complex data transformations to generate high-value data

- Data science and machine learning solutions that are leveraged by data scientists for ad hoc exploratory analysis

- A cloud data warehouse that serves this high-value data to BI use cases and data analysts

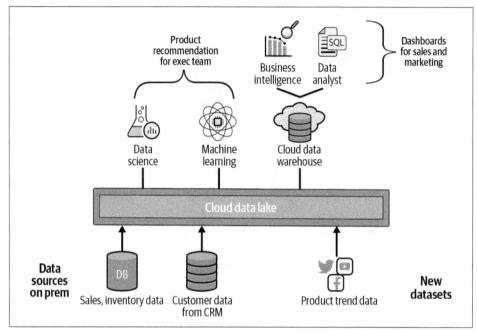

Figure 3-3. Proposed cloud data lake architecture for Klodars Corporation

The deliverable for their project consists of the following phases:

Phase 1: Ingestion
Load data into the data lake. Set up automated pipelines to take daily backups of the operational databases and CRM system in the data lake. Store data for the past 90 days.

Phase 2: Processing
This consists of two phases that can run in parallel:

Process BI data
Run processing pipelines to refresh data daily into the cloud data warehouse. Validate with feedback from data analysts on sales and marketing teams.

Advanced scenarios
Develop product recommendation models based on data from the operational databases and CRM system, leveraging data scientists.

Phase 3: Limited release

This phase involves the release of the data lake platform to select customers from the sales, marketing, and executive teams while the on-premises implementation is still running. This helps catch issues early and iterate based on customer feedback.

Phase 4: Release to production

This involves the release of the data lake to all customers at the Klodars Corporation. At this point, both the on-premises and the cloud platforms are running in parallel.

Phase 5: Turn off on-premises dashboards

Once the data lake implementation is successful on the cloud, the dashboards running on premises for the analysis will be turned off.

Implement the Cloud Data Lake

In this phase, the architecture will be implemented according to the project plan. This phase involves key decisions around choice of cloud providers and follows the best practices for infrastructure. Given that the choice of cloud providers goes beyond technical reasons, we will not go into details here. Some important considerations in this phase that apply to all cloud providers include the following:

Set up and manage your cloud identities

A key fundamental step to getting started on the cloud is to create your identity management system on the cloud provider. If you have an identity management system on premises, cloud providers allow you to federate your on-premises identities to the cloud.

Set up your subscriptions

A subscription is required to create resources (Iaas, PaaS, or SaaS offered on the cloud). A subscription also has access controls associated with it; you can assign your cloud-managed identities to specific roles (owner, contributor, etc.) for your subscription.

Create environments

It's highly recommend that you create separate environments for development (that your developers can use to test their code), preproduction (access to all developers and select customers), and production. I also recommend that you use separate subscriptions for the different environments to keep them isolated from one another. If you have a presence in multiple regions that are subject to different requirements, you can create separate environments for each region, such as North America or Europe.

Choose your services

Cloud providers offer a variety of services (IaaS, PaaS, or SaaS) for your cloud data lake architecture. Take the time to talk to your cloud providers and make the right choices depending on the opportunity, business needs, and cost.

Invest in automation and observability

In addition to implementing the data lake itself, ensure you have the required automation to create and manage resources on demand. Given that you will be paying for what you use on the cloud (as opposed to having hardware around all the time), the automation will ensure that you can create and delete resources on demand to help manage your costs. Similarly, make sure that you have logging and monitoring on the cloud so that you can monitor the health of your systems.

For more information, you can check out the documentation on getting started by the top cloud providers, AWS (*https://oreil.ly/N1N-_*), Microsoft Azure (*https://oreil.ly/KVxG9*), and Google Cloud (*https://oreil.ly/DMGmZ*).

Release and Operationalize

In this phase, the project plan is appropriately resourced, tracked, implemented, and released to production, so the on-premises implementation can be turned off with confidence.

Some considerations for this phases include the following:

- Consider early and frequent releases to a limited audience to ensure that you can catch issues earlier and iterate based on feedback.

- Ensure that you have releases starting in the development environment, and tested in the preproduction environment before they release to production.

The popular cloud providers have tools and platforms that help with observability and automation, such as Lake Formation (*https://oreil.ly/bjWQF*) for automation and CloudWatch (*https://oreil.ly/9q2tf*) for observability from AWS, Azure Resource Manager (*https://oreil.ly/MVaKH*) for automation and Azure Monitor (*https://oreil.ly/WkFsK*) for observability on Microsoft Azure, and Resource Manager (*https://oreil.ly/9D9SY*) for automation and Cloud Monitoring (*https://oreil.ly/d0Edi*) for observability on Google Cloud.

At the end of this phase, you will have an operational data lake ready that you can test in your developer, preproduction, and production environments. In the next sections, we will talk about the specifics of setting up the data lake architecture, which includes organizing the data, managing and governing the data lake, and managing costs.

Organizing Data in Your Data Lake

Once you have the infrastructure pieces set up and tested end to end, the very next step is to ingest data. Before you ingest data into the data lake, it's important to ensure that you have a strategy to organize data in the data lake. When you set up a kitchen, you need to know in which cabinets to store your china, your pots and pans, and your coffee. You would make sure that the pots and pans are more accessible to the stovetop and that the coffee, sugar, and creamers are stored together. To understand data organization within the data lake, let's take a look at the lifecycle of data in the data lake.

A Day in the Life of Data

Data is first ingested from various sources in its raw natural state into the data lake. It is then cleansed and prepared for future processing, such as applying a schema, removing duplicates, removing null values, and fixing them with defaults in some cases. At the end of this data-prep phase, data adheres to a tabular structure as is defined by the data-prep code. As a next step, this data is aggregated, joined, and filtered to extract high-value data—this phase is curation. In addition to the data that follows this lifecycle, consumers like data scientists can bring in their own datasets for exploratory analysis.

This lifecycle is an important point for you to remember because it is an indicator of a different pattern. The most common pattern of loading data for analysis in previous decades was ETL: extract, transform, and load. Data was extracted from its source, transformed to adhere to a specific structure, and loaded into a store (Hadoop filesystem or data warehouse). If a signal in the data was lost as part of this transformation, it was not trivial, and in some cases, it was impossible to retrieve that signal from the source again. Further, with innovations in cloud infrastructure and silicon, storage is getting cheaper and cheaper over time. This combination of increased value in data along with inexpensive storage has given rise to a new pattern called ELT: extract, load, and transform. In this pattern, data is extracted from its source, loaded into the data lake, and transformed later with data processing.

Data Lake Zones

Following this lifecycle of data, data will be organized into different zones within your data lake. Let's now take a look at these zones in detail. Figure 3-4 provides a visual of each of these zones, and in this section, we'll walk through each of them.

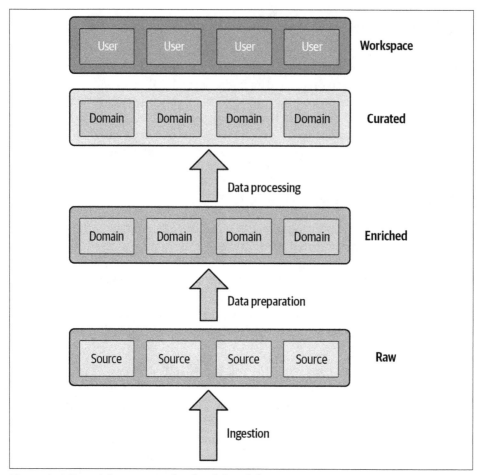

Figure 3-4. Data lake zones in the cloud data lake

The data in the data lake can be segmented into the following zones depending on the stage of processing and the value density packed into the data:

Raw data (Bronze) zone

This zone contains data in its natural state as it was ingested from its source. This zone has data with the lowest-value density (i.e., high signal-to-noise ratio), and this data is ready to go through various transformations to generate valuable insights.

Enriched data (Silver) zone

This zone contains the transformed version of the raw data, adhering to a structure as it is relevant for your business scenario. At this point, the value density is low to medium; however, there is a certain level of guarantee for the data to adhere to a schema or a structure.

Curated data (Gold) zone

This zone contains data with the highest-value density. The data in this zone is generated by applying transformations to enriched data.

Workspace data zone

This zone is provisioned to consumers of the data lake to bring their own datasets. There is no specific guarantee for this data zone; think of this as a scratch pad that you provision in the data lake.

Let's now take a look at these sections in detail:

Raw data (Bronze) zone

This is the section of the data lake in which data first lands from external sources. In the ELT pattern we talked about, this is the data that is extracted from the source and loaded into the data lake storage. Data is ingested from various sources, such as on-premises systems, social media, external open datasets, and so forth. Data can be ingested either in a scheduled fashion (think bulk uploads) or in real time (think events). Data in this zone has minimal guarantee or structure, semantics, and value. The most common pattern is that this ingestion is typically controlled by a select set of teams and not open to everyone. Data in this zone will be organized by the ingestion source as well as by the timestamp of the data. In a typical data lake scenario, most data has time associated with it (e.g., Twitter feeds for a particular day, server logs from a particular hour of a day, etc.). So this zone will typically be organized by the source, and within the source by the time; this time structure indicates the freshness of the data.

Enriched data (Silver) zone

Raw data as it is ingested into the data lake doesn't quite conform to a specific structure or format. As we saw in "A Word on Variety of Data" on page 23, data ingested into the data lake could be structured, semistructured, or unstructured. The data is then cleansed and processed to fit into a tabular structure; this process is called *data preparation* or *enrichment* or *data cooking*. Three key things typically happen in this step:

Schema definition

The schema essentially is the definition of a structure that the data adheres to—that is, meaning is given to different parts of the data, making it a tabular structure with column definitions.

Data cleansing

Once the schema is defined, there may be some parts of the data that don't adhere to the schema. For example, if the schema indicates that the fifth field of your CSV file is a zip code, then this step ensures that the values adhere to a zip code format (XXXXX or XXXXX-XXXX) and if they don't, either removes it or fills it with legitimate values (e.g., looks up the zip code from the address).

Optimizations
> Once the data adheres to a tabular structure, it is also important to prepare the data to be optimized for the most common consumption patterns. The most common pattern is for data to be written once and read many times. For example, if you have a sales database, the most common queries on this data tend to be for region-specific sales information or trends over time. In this step, data is converted into a format and reorganized to be friendly for the most common queries. Typically, a columnar format like Parquet, which we saw in "Data formats" on page 45, is selected to be optimized for queries.

> This data is used more broadly by the different teams, data scientists, and, in some cases, business analysts as well for more ad hoc analysis. Data in this zone is organized into domains, or units that the various consumers can understand, and is published in a catalog (we will talk more about this in "Introduction to Data Governance" on page 78).

Curated data (Gold) zone
> The curated data zone has the highest-value data in the data lake and critical datasets that power key business dashboards. Think of the data in this zone as a digest or a summary of the value in the data, the key insights. Data in this zone is processed by performing aggregations, filtering, correlating data from different datasets, and other complex calculations that provide the key insights into solutions for business problems. The data in this zone uses data in the curated zone as its source, along with other data sources occasionally. Data in this zone needs to adheres to the highest standards in terms of data quality, given its broad impact to the business.

> Curated data is mostly used by business analysts and powers dashboards that are leveraged by key business decision makers. Additionally, this data is published in a catalog and is organized by the business units and the domains it is relevant to.

Workspace or sandbox zone (optional)
> As we discussed, the data that is present in the raw, enriched, and curated zones is largely managed by a select set of data engineers or data platform teams. However, there are datasets that consumers would like to bring, either for exploratory analysis or to test the waters. This data can be organized into units that are specifically provisioned for the user (think of this like a scratch pad). Data here adheres to no specific standard or quality and is essentially available for any free-form use.

Figure 3-5 illustrates the data organization at Klodars Corporation.

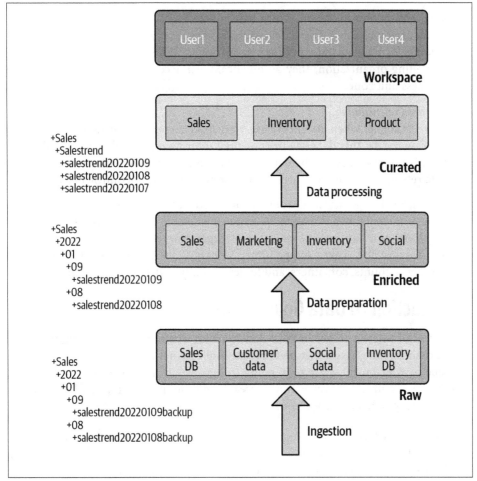

Figure 3-5. Data organization within the data lake at Klodars Corporation

Organization Mechanisms

Although not a strong requirement, it is a good practice to organize your data in a way that aligns with the usage patterns. As we discussed in "Data Lake Zones" on page 73, data goes through a certain lifecycle within the data lake, and you could align your organization by grouping data together as zones. This organization is very helpful as the data and usage continues to grow in your data lake, as it certainly will. The organization mechanism comes in handy for many reasons, including the following:

Control access to the data

As an example, access to the data in the raw zone is typically locked down to the data platform team, and you help manage access. When a new employee joins the marketing organization, they automatically get access to data in the marketing business unit zone.

Manage data retention

As an example, when you provision workspace zones to your users for bringing their own data, this data has the potential to grow uncontrollably since the data itself is not managed by the data platform team. The data platform team can set data retention policies for specific zones to manage this uncontrollable growth.

The data lake storage services from major cloud providers offer different ways to organize your data zones. Amazon S3 (*https://aws.amazon.com/s3*) and GCS (*https://oreil.ly/pJD0z*) provide buckets as units of organizing data that you can leverage. Microsoft Azure Data Lake Storage (*https://oreil.ly/VQ9nX*) offers a native filesystem with storage accounts, containers, and folders as units of data organization.

Introduction to Data Governance

Regardless of where you are in your data journey, whether you are taking your first steps or you already have a mature data lake implementation, the amount of data and its value to your business are only going to increase. In the words of Uncle Ben in *Spider-man*, "With great power comes great responsibility." Let's take a look at some of the challenges that can arise from managing data:

- The data that you collect could have personal or business-critical information, such as the person's name and address, or trade secrets, which in the wrong hands could potentially harm the person or business. Huge enterprises like Yahoo (*https://oreil.ly/Oi_iO*), Starwood Marriott Hotels (*https://oreil.ly/FWr8W*), Alibaba (*https://oreil.ly/sGlC1*), and so many more have had to deal with data breaches over the years.

- The errors in the balance and completeness of your data could skew your analysis, resulting in building nonideal experiences for your users. In 2016, Microsoft unveiled a conversational AI chatbot (*https://oreil.ly/gtFYd*) that quickly learned to tweet racist and sexist messages because of the datasets that taught the bot.

- As the data grows in your data lake, along with the usage of the data, management and discovery of these datasets becomes extremely important. Without them, you run the risk of turning your data lake into a *data swamp*. To understand this better, think of that cluttered closet (or room or garage or attic) where after a point, you have no idea what is even there, and you never go near it until it's moving time.

- There are a rising number of data privacy regulations, such as the General Data Protection Regulation (GDPR) (*https://gdpr-info.eu*), the California Consumer Privacy Act (CCPA) (*https://oag.ca.gov/privacy/ccpa*), and many others, that you need to pay attention to while operating your cloud data lake.

 As *Data Governance: The Definitive Guide* (*https://oreil.ly/L4sTR*) by Evren Eryurek, Uri Gilad, Valliappa Lakshmanan, Anita Kibunguchy-Grant, and Jessi Ashdown (O'Reilly) states, "Ultimately, the purpose of data governance is to build trust in data. Data governance is valuable to the extent that it adds to stakeholders' trust in the data—specifically, in how that data is collected, analyzed, published, or used."

Actors Involved in Data Governance

Data governance is an umbrella term that refers to the technologies, tools, and processes that ensure that data used by an organization is secure, accessible, usable, and compliant. There are four primary actors involved in the data governance of an organization. Data governance tools are designed to meet the needs of one or more of these actors. Note that the actors are not always human users but can also be applications or services. Further, the same team or organization can play the role of one or more of these actors:

Data officers
> This group essentially manages the definition and requirements for what it means for the data to be trusted and ensures that the requirements are met with periodic audits and reviews. This involves defining and managing controls for things like data sharing requirements, data retention policies, and compliance regulations that need to be met for the data estate. They set the bar for data governance.

Data engineers
> These are the actors who implement the data lake architecture. They provision and set up the various services, manage the identities for the actors, and put the right set of technologies and processes in place to ensure that the data and associated insights have the required amount of trust. In other words, they implement and manage the infrastructure and technologies and ensure that the implementation meets the requirements defined by the data officers. They leverage various tool sets to understand the different stages of processing that the data went through, a process known as tracking the lineage of the data, and guarantee the quality and consistency of the data. They also play a key role in providing collateral and evidence for the reviews and audits.

If you have heard the term *master data management* (MDM), this essentially refers to data about the data assets in the organization, including location, customer, products, and so on. This is different from the metadata that we saw in Chapter 2, which is data about the data in terms of describing the schema.

Data producers

These are one segment of the users of the data lake. As the name suggests, data producers bring data into your data estate. This data could be raw (ingested from external and internal sources), enriched (prepared/cooked data that is in a tabular form), curated (summary/digest with high-value insights), or ad hoc datasets that are produced and consumed by data scientists. Data producers care deeply about ensuring that the data adheres to a certain level of quality depending on the type, and they want to ensure that they are aware of how the data needs to be locked down or opened up to the rest of the organization in terms of managing access. They need to adhere to the tools and processes set by the data officers and data engineers and not attempt to circumvent the guardrails.

Data consumers

These are the other segment of users of the data lake. As with anything else, a product is valuable only when there are customers using it. Data is no exception. Whether they use dashboards, queryable tables, or ad hoc datasets, data consumers are anyone who consumes the data or insights. The data producers have control over who gets to use the data, and data consumers actually consume this data either as is or for further processing. For example, in the data curation process, the set of users or applications ends up consuming the enriched data and producing the curated data.

Figure 3-6 provides a very simplistic overview of some of the top-of-mind concerns for the various actors who interact with the data estate—in this case, the data lake.

A lot of tools and automations are available for these different actors to enable better data governance and follow best practices. Having said that, you can also conduct data governance with manual operations. Data governance can be categorized into the tasks that can be accomplished either with tools and automation or with manually enforced processes.

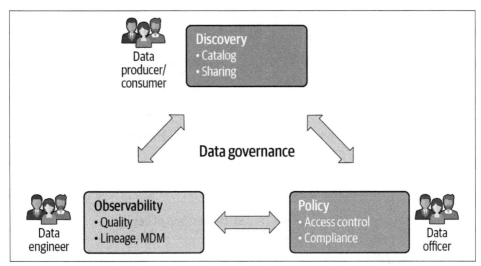

Figure 3-6. Data governance components

Data Classification

Data governance always starts with the data officers, who work on defining the requirements and controls for the data that can be collected, stored, and processed.

Data type refers to the types of data or assets that the organization uses. The data in your data lake needs to be tagged with one or more of these types. The data type itself, also referred to as an *infotype*, has a singular meaning associated with it, such as data containing a first name or zip code. These infotypes are organized into data classes. For example, name and address fall into the personally identifiable information (PII) data class, and a credit card number falls into the financial information data class.

Figure 3-7 illustrates this hierarchy with an example.

Policies are rules and restrictions that are applicable to the classes of data. For instance, your policy could be that consumers' PII data must always be collected after the consumer consents to it once they clearly understand how your organization plans to use that information.

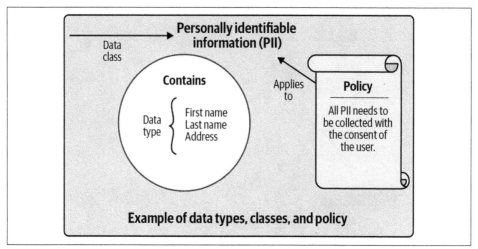

Figure 3-7. Data types, classes, and policy example

If your enterprise handles sensitive data such as PII or financial information, you will need to comply with policies and regulations that are enforced by your organization or even sometimes by governments. You will need to prove to the regulator (whoever sets those regulations) that you have the policies in place; this is usually accomplished via audits. It is recommended that you define these policies and have records of your handling completed in a planned manner to avoid fire drills during reviews and audits.

To ensure that your data complies with the policies, the data in your data lake needs to be classified—associated with the class and the type—so you can apply the relevant policies. Cloud services like Amazon Macie (*https://oreil.ly/aMk7f*) leverage machine learning to provide automated classification of data in your data lake and work on structured, unstructured, and semistructured data.

Metadata Management, Data Catalog, and Data Sharing

Metadata refers to the technical data that describes the format and fields of the data stored in the data lake as well as other data that has more business context for the datasets. For the purposes of this book, we will focus on the technical metadata. For instance, for an employee table, the metadata has the description. The first column is the first name, which is an array of strings, followed by another array of strings that represents the last name. The next field is the age, which is an integer between 15 and 100.

A *data catalog* is a system that stores this metadata and can be published for the rest of the organization. As an analogy, in a library with a lot of books, it's impossible to find the book you want without a catalog, where you can search for a book by the title or author. Similarly, data consumers can leverage the data catalog to look for the tables they have access to, either with the table name or with certain key fields. You might search for all the tables about employees, for example. The key thing to remember here is that one data catalog can hold data from various data sources, the data lake, the data warehouse, and any other storage systems. Figure 3-8 illustrates this concept.

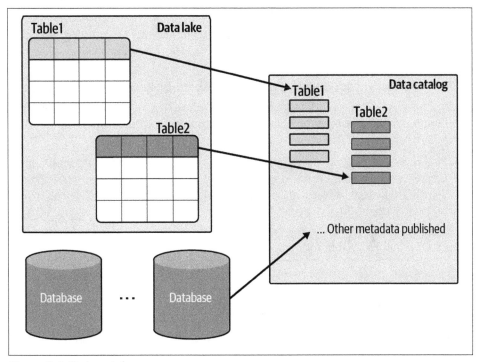

Figure 3-8. Data catalog

Once key datasets and high-value insights are available to an organization, there may be other consumers either within the organization or, in some cases, even outside the organization. In other words, data is like a product that can be shared and monetized with a larger audience. *Data sharing* is an emerging capability of data governance where datasets in a data lake or data warehouse can be shared with an audience inside or outside an organization, with the consumer paying the data producer for the data access. Data catalogs make these scenarios much easier to implement.

Data Access Management

When we talk about data discoverability via catalogs and data sharing, we must ensure that the right set of actors has access to the right data, and more importantly, that actors don't have access to other data. A key part of data governance is access management, where there is a set of capabilities that lets the actors manage data at various levels, from access to the data stored to access to the data through other applications like data sharing or through the warehouse.

I would like to explain this concept as a ringed approach to data access management:

- At the very inner core, there is access to the data itself, which is a data lake storage–level security model that helps you lock access to the storage itself.

- The next layer involves access to the computational engines running on top of the data lake storage, either via the ETL processes, the data warehouse, or the dashboards.

- The next layer involves boundaries at your cloud system level, which controls the visibility and accessibility of your cloud resources or your data across a network boundary, such as regional access restrictions on what data needs to stay in a region versus what can be transacted across regions.

- Finally, you can use comprehensive data security tools, such as Apache Ranger (*https://ranger.apache.org*), to apply advanced rules and policies across the data in your multiple data stores (e.g., data tagged as PII must not have access to anyone other than the HR department).

Figure 3-9 illustrates this approach.

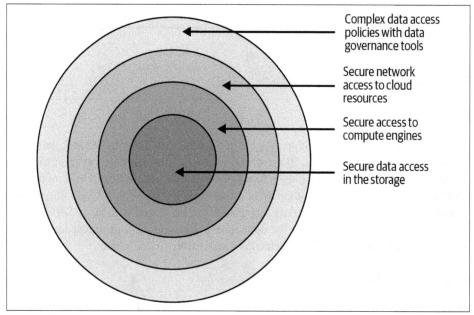

Figure 3-9. Approach to access management

Data Quality and Observability

Given the criticality of data to running a business, the quality of data has grown to be as important, if not more important, than the quality of the code. Whether it is an outage that blocks critical news like COVID-19 data (*https://oreil.ly/eW1Xo*) or a wrong award announcement like the embarrassing announcement that *La La Land* won the Oscar in 2017 (*https://oreil.ly/-sX94*), mistakes in data have a ripple effect downstream.

Organizations are increasingly relying on measuring and monitoring data quality as a best practice, and this is one growing area of investment in the data lake space. Although it is out of scope for this book, I recommend that you check out other resources on data quality and data observability for more in-depth coverage of the concepts and learn more about the available tool sets you can leverage for your data quality and observability solutions. I will provide an overview of the basic concepts and approaches to data observability in this section.

In *Data Quality Fundamentals* (*https://oreil.ly/5L_mc*) by Barr Moses, Lior Gavish, and Molly Vorwerck (O'Reilly), there is a succinct definition of the five pillars of data observability, or the attributes that need to be measured to ensure data quality in your data lake architecture. This is a great starting point for how to think about data observability.

Especially in a cloud data lake architecture, there is a disparate set of components that load data into the data lake storage and process data to generate high-value insights, and there is yet another set of components that draws the dashboards. One component is not quite aware of the others. Hence, data observability is of critical importance in building this common understanding across the components in a data lake by taking a data-centric approach.

Paraphrasing from the book, the five pillars of data observability are as follows:

Freshness
> *Freshness* is an indicator of the recency of the data. When was the last time this data was refreshed? As an example, we talked in earlier chapters about a common pattern of having daily uploads of data from the operational datastore into the data lake. The freshness attribute indicates how fresh this update was, so if last night's data upload failed, then you are clear that the reports are based on data that is two days old.

Distribution
> *Distribution* is an indicator of the acceptable ranges or values of the data. This lets you define acceptable ranges for the data. Often, when the charts in your dashboards looked abnormal, you would wonder if the data was highlighting a genuine problem or if the data was just simply wrong or broken. Ensuring that you have acceptable ranges for the data helps you know that when the data

goes above or below the acceptable ranges, you have a data problem rather than a real issue with the trends. As an example, when your recent sales data has not yet arrived, you might see $0 sales, when it is unlikely that there were no sales. Similarly, if you see that your sales suddenly jumped 500% compared to the normal range, you'll know you need to investigate whether this is a genuine reason to celebrate or there might be some duplicate processing that double counted the sales data.

Volume

Volume is an indicator of the acceptable size of the data. Similar to the distribution, this indicates the acceptable levels of the size of the data, and any data outside of this range is possibly an indicator of the data levels. As an example, when your data table typically has 10,000 rows, and after the day's processing you see 10 rows or 5 million rows, then you get that cue to investigate further.

Schema

As we have seen earlier, *schema* refers to the description of the data in terms of the structure of the data and the semantic definitions. If an upstream component changes the schema, then one or more of the fields might disappear, breaking the downstream scenarios. Tracking changes to the schema itself helps us understand its effect on the downstream components and isolate the changes to the impact.

Lineage

In the simplest terms, *lineage* can be described as a dependency graph between the producers and consumers of the data. For a given dataset, data lineage describes how the data is generated and which components consume it. When there is an error, data lineage provides the bread crumbs that you can trace back to the other components you need to investigate.

It is recommended that organizations invest in automation to measure these pillars to ensure that the data is of acceptable quality and that the data lake can provide guarantees in terms of service-level agreements (SLAs) on how well the data meets the standards.

Data Quality and Observability

With Lior Gavish, Cofounder and CTO, and Molly Vorwerck, Content and Communications, Monte Carlo Corporation (https://www.montecarlodata.com)

Anything that is created by humans breaks, sometimes in an unpredictable way.

Just as Datadog or New Relic supports observability of code and services, there is a need for minimizing unpredictability in data pipelines. Data quality is increasingly important as organizations continue to rely on data for critical business decisions.

Data quality in data lakes is more complex than in structured data warehouses because of the diversity of data and the myriad computational engines.

In a data warehouse, there is a single stack of compute and storage together, and there is a single point or surface of usage. In a data lake, there are many different computational engines, such as real-time streaming and batch ingestion, Spark or Hadoop processing engines, and query engines like Presto, all running on the storage. It is hard to know where your data assets are coming from, what engines are modifying them, and who is consuming them; mapping all of this together is key to ensuring data quality. This complexity is only exacerbated by the high scale at which a data lake operates.

A useful framework for data reliability is to ensure there is a measurable metric for the five key pillars: data freshness, distribution, volume, schema, and lineage. The implementation of this framework is key to understanding, measuring, and mitigating data quality issues. Data lakes have accelerated the need for data quality to be top of mind, not just an afterthought, to ensure trust is guaranteed for the data and insights.

Given that data lakes store a wider variety of data, it could get very expensive and laborious to implement data quality for *all* the data in the data lake. A highly recommended approach is to start your data quality initiative by identifying the high-priority datasets and defining SLAs and service-level objectives (SLOs) for those datasets in terms of the five data quality pillars. These SLAs and SLOs become the goals and also serve as requirements for implementing data quality for your data lake. Not all data is equally important, and this prioritization is key to ensuring that you can offer data quality while also maintaining development agility.

Data Governance at Klodars Corporation

Alice and her team understand the importance of data governance for their data platform architecture and set out to make the following changes:

- They leverage a data catalog based on the open source Apache Atlas (*https:// atlas.apache.org*) to curate and publish the metadata for data in their enriched and curated zones.

- They classify data in the Sales and Customer tables with the right classes—PII, financial information, and so on—and data types and ensure that the data catalog has information about this data classification.

- Given that they don't require the actual PII information for their scenarios, they write a PII scrubber to ensure that the PII data is masked (a unique hash for the value is stored instead of the value in plain text). The result is that the data analysts can still look at information for unique users without seeing their personal information.

- From a security and access control perspective, they do the following:
  - They implement data lake storage security so that access to raw data is locked down to just the platform team and access to enriched data and curated datasets is read-only for the business analysts and data scientists in their organizations. The data scientists and business analysts have read and write access to the workspaces provisioned for them but can't see other users' workspaces unless they choose to share explicitly.
  - They ensure that the product and executive teams have access to the dashboards and that the data scientists have access to all of the data science computational frameworks. The ingest pipeline and data-prep pipeline are strictly locked down to the data engineering team.
  - They implement a data governance solution that has the data catalog as well as policy and access management across both the data lake and the data warehouse data.

Figure 3-10 shows the implementation of data governance by Klodars Corporation.

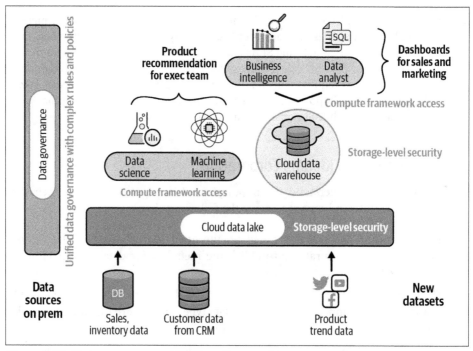

Figure 3-10. Data governance at Klodars Corporation

Data Governance Wrap-Up

Putting all these concepts together, I will summarize the approach to data governance as a series of steps you can take to build trust in the data with your customers of the data lake:

1. Understand the data governance policies that the data officers are experts at as well as the requirements of your customers: the data producers and data consumers. These requirements govern the implementation of data governance by your data engineers.

2. Understand and classify the data within your data lake to ensure that you know what policies apply to what datasets.

3. Build a data catalog to manage the metadata that helps with understanding and discovering the datasets that are available. This makes it easier for your data producers and consumers to publish and find the available datasets. This also helps the data engineers implement data access and governance policies and enables the data officers to audit and review the datasets for compliance. You can also leverage data-sharing capabilities to control and manage how data is shared.

4. Manage data access at various levels—at the data layer, the compute engine layer, and the network layer—and set customized, automated data policies to ensure that you control and restrict data access to comply with the access policies.

5. Invest in the right levels of data observability to ensure you have reliable monitoring to help identify and debug data quality issues.

Manage Data Lake Costs

One of the biggest value propositions of a cloud data lake architecture is the lower cost. These are the main drivers of this lower cost:

- *No cost to maintain datacenters and maintenance*—the cloud providers take care of this.

- *Pay-for-consumption* model on the cloud that lets you pay only for what you consume, as opposed to having hardware around all the time.

- *Decoupled compute and storage* that lets you scale your compute and storage independently, thereby ensuring that your larger storage needs don't have a corresponding increase in storage costs.

This provides the flexibility for you to bring in more data and light up more scenarios on your data lake without exploding the costs. While the per-unit cost is lower on the data lake, there are some factors that increase data lake costs that you should be aware of so you can balance business objectives with your implementation:

- Cloud services offer lower costs because you pay for what you consume. However, this entails an implicit understanding that you have the cloud resources running on-demand and that you shut them down when they are not used. If you do not manage this on-demand provisioning and shutting down of your cloud resources, you end up leaving them running all the time, and this *consumption model might not apply* in your case.

- As we saw earlier, cloud data lake architecture has a disaggregated compute and storage design, which optimizes cost because you can scale compute and storage independently depending on your need. However, this design also requires awareness of the *transaction costs* for data transferred between services, such as compute transacting with storage service.

- In a cloud architecture, there are no network costs for transactions within the cloud resources that are provisioned within the same region. Similarly, there are no costs to ingress data into the cloud from other sources, such as your on-premises systems. However, there are *network costs* when you transfer data across regions or when you egress data—transfer data from the cloud to your components outside the cloud, such as your on-premises systems.

- With the promise of data lake storage being cheap, there is an opportunity to bring in any and all kinds of data, even when you don't have immediate use for it. This potentially has the side effect of causing *uncontrolled growth of data*, making the data lake a data swamp, which drives up the costs as well.

- The cloud services offer rich feature sets for data management, data durability, and performance. These *features of cloud services* drive up costs when chosen in an unoptimized fashion.

In this section, let's take a broader look at these factors by understanding how cloud interactions work and how they drive your costs. We'll also take a look at how you can optimize your costs with careful design considerations.

Demystifying Data Lake Costs on the Cloud

Your cloud data lake implementation consists primarily of the following key components:

Data storage
> Either the data lake storage or, in some cases, the data warehouse where the data is stored and organized. The billing model here has two key pivots: cost of data stored and cost of transactions.

Compute engine
> The services where the data is processed and transformed, essentially the calculator engines. These could be big data frameworks like Spark engines IaaS or even SaaS. The cost component here primarily relates to the utilization of the compute, such as price per compute unit (that the compute engine defines) based on how much CPU and memory are used and price per core per hour utilized.

Software cost
> You pay a subscription (typically per month) to use the software.

Network cost
> The cost of transferring data over the wire, especially for data that is transferred across regions or out of the cloud (egress cost). The price is typically for data transferred (per gigabyte).

Figure 3-11 illustrates these costs as they relate to a data lake architecture.

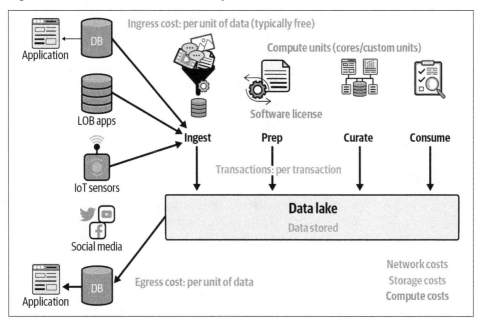

Figure 3-11. Data lake costs

These building blocks of costs can manifest themselves in different ways that affect the total cost of your data lake. For example, although you know you are paying for data stored, the exact cost depends on how you have designed your storage system. Following are some factors that contribute to the variable storage costs:

Storage tier

Tiers of storage have different costs. For example, a hot/standard tier costs more than an archive tier for data stored at rest, but it costs less for transactions. So data is best stored in the standard tier if it's highly transacted and in an archival tier for cold storage—that is, for data retention purposes only without transactions, like data that needs to meet a retention policy.

Data protection and durability features

Data protection features like versioning and backup and redundant storage features like cross-region replication offer much higher durability for your data; however, they do come with a price tag for the extra copies. Given that all data is not equal in your data lake, it's better to use these features for your high-value data.

Transaction costs

There are two specific transactions you need to pay attention to: any networking costs, specifically associated with cross-region egress or egress out of your cloud into an on-premises system, and transaction costs for transfer of data between different services. For storage transactions, the cost of transactions is calculated by the number of transactions, so transferring the same amount of data (e.g., 1 GB) with many small files (e.g., 1 KB) would cost more than transferring larger files (a few hundred megabytes).

Building this key understanding of the cost drivers of the cloud data lake system is necessary for you to optimize the costs based on your needs.

Data Lake Cost Strategy

A good data lake cost strategy always starts with understanding the business need, architecture, data, and, most importantly, your customers. Figure 3-12 shows the key factors you need to understand about your data lake.

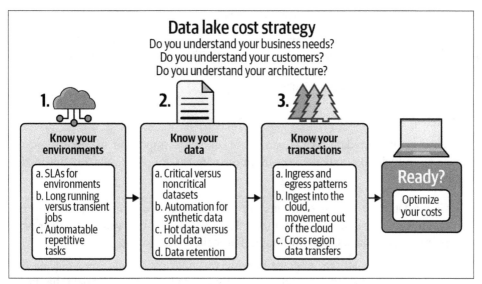

Figure 3-12. Data lake cost strategy

Let's look at the key aspects of the data lake architecture and the associated strategies for cost management.

Data Lake Environments and Associated Costs

In your data lake architecture, just like in your coding environments, there are different environments: dev environments for your data developers to work on, preproduction environments for end-to-end testing, and production environments that support your customers. You need to understand the usage and the SLAs you promise for these environments so you can configure them with the appropriate level of configurations. For example, for your dev environments, you might not need very powerful compute cores given that the kinds of workloads running there are to verify functionality. Your stress-testing environment might need a lot of cores because you are pushing the limits of your system, but your stress tests could run weekly, and you don't need to keep them around all the time. Your production environments need to meet your SLAs for your customers and cannot compromise on availability or performance. Similarly, knowing the nature of your jobs determines what environments need to be up all the time versus what can be generated on demand. For example, the clusters for notebooks that data scientists work on could be started on demand, whereas the clusters that power your critical business dashboards need to be up all the time. For on-demand clusters, having automation in place would help spin up and shut down resources on demand. Automation is also useful for generating synthetic data on demand for your use cases instead of storing data.

Quick Tip for On-Demand Resources

Cloud services have serverless capabilities where you can focus on submitting your job or query without having to worry about managing resources or clusters. These are worth investigating for your on-demand jobs.

Cost strategy based on data

Not all data in your data lake is equivalent, and it is important to understand the value, reproducibility, and the consumption patterns for your data for optimizing your data costs:

- Cloud data lake storage solutions provide reservation options where, if you can commit to a certain size of data (e.g., 100 TB at least), you will get a lower price point for your data. Check this out if that makes sense to you.

- Cloud data lake storage systems provide varying *tiers of data storage*. Data that needs to be frequently transacted is referred to as *hot data*, while data that needs to be stored but not transacted frequently is referred to as *cold data*. For cold data, use an archive tier that costs way less for data storage but is high for transactions. The archive tiers also have a minimum retention period that you need to pay attention to. Use a standard tier for data that is highly transacted.

- Cloud data lake storage systems also offer *high data durability* features, such as versioning: multiple copies of data are stored so you can protect against data corruption, your data can be replicated across multiple regions for resilience to disasters, and your data can be stored in hardened back-up systems to offer data protection. These features are ideal for critical datasets but are not necessary for noncritical datasets where you can tolerate corruption or deletion.

- Cloud data storage systems have *data retention policies* that you can implement so that data is deleted automatically after a certain period. It is common practice to take daily or weekly or <insert your favorite periodicity> snapshots of data from various sources to be loaded into your data lake. This could easily spike your costs and end up making your data lake a data swamp. Setting retention policies according to the lifetime of your data ensures that your data lake is decluttered.

Transactions and impact on costs

The transaction costs, whether they are network egress costs or data storage transaction costs, in most cases come as a surprise to the data lake consumer and are often ignored. The catch is that these transaction costs are also the hardest to model. There are two factors that you need to pay attention to for transactions:

- The number of transactions
- The data transferred

The best way to understand and optimize your transaction costs is to run a scaled proof of concept (PoC) that is representative of your production workloads. It is also a best practice to ensure that you avoid antipatterns such as small files and make them at least a few hundred megabytes per file. In addition to saving costs, this improves the scalability and performance of your data lake solution. We will discuss this in more detail in Chapter 4. While this might not be feasible for all data in the data lake, you could address this for data in the enriched and curated zones. For example, IoT data tends to be a few bytes or a few kilobytes and is stored in the raw data lake zone. However, a conscious step in data preparation could be to aggregate this data into a larger file to optimize for transactions.

Summary

In this chapter, we dove deep into the implementation details of a cloud data lake. We first took a look at how to start planning the implementation of your cloud data lake. We then talked about the heart of the data lake, the data: strategies to organize and manage data into zones based on the natural lifecycle of data. Next, we got an overview of data governance to help manage the discoverability, access, and sharing constraints of data in the data lake. Finally, we addressed the factors that contribute to data lake costs and strategized to optimize the costs. My goal for this chapter was to help you build an understanding of the basic concepts of designing a data lake architecture. With this understanding, you will be able to design a data lake architecture by picking the right cloud offerings that suit your needs and implement it with the right configurations. If you don't know what the right configurations are, refer to this chapter, and frame your requirements to the cloud service provider or the ISV. In the next two chapters, I will talk about the concepts and principles of architecting your data lake for scale and performance, respectively.

CHAPTER 4

Scalable Data Lakes

If you change the way you look at things, the things you look at change.

—Wayne Dyer

After reading the first three chapters, you should have all you need to get your data lake architecture up and running on the cloud, at a reasonable cost profile for your organization. Theoretically, you also have the first set of use cases and scenarios successfully running in production. Your data lake is so successful that the demand for more scenarios is now higher, and you are busy serving the needs of your new customers. Your business is booming, and your data estate is growing rapidly. As they say in business, going from zero to one is a different challenge than going from one to one hundred or from one hundred to one thousand. To ensure your design is also scalable and continues to perform as your data and the use cases grow, it's important to realize the various factors that affect the scale and performance of your data lake. Contrary to popular opinion, scale and performance are not always a trade-off with costs, but they very much go hand in hand. In this chapter, we will take a closer look at these considerations as well as strategies to optimize your data lake for scale while continuing to optimize for costs. Once again, we will be using Klodars Corporation, a fictitious organization, to illustrate our strategies. We will build on these fundamentals to focus on performance in Chapter 5.

A Sneak Peek into Scalability

Scale and performance are terms you have likely seen sprinkled generously into product pitches and marketing materials. What do they actually mean, and why are they important? To understand this better, let's first look at the definition of scalability. In Chapter 5, we will dive deep into the performance aspects.

What Is Scalability?

The best definition of *scalability* that I have ever come across is from Werner Vogels's blog (*https://oreil.ly/M5kVr*). Vogels was the CTO of Amazon, which hosts one of the largest hyperscale systems on the planet. According to his blog, the definition of scalability goes like this:

> A service is said to be scalable if when we increase the resources in a system, it results in increased performance in a manner proportional to resources added. An always-on service is said to be scalable if adding resources to facilitate redundancy does not result in a loss of performance.

This concept of scale is very important because as your needs and usage grow, it is important to have an architecture that can guarantee the same experience to your customers without degradation in performance. To illustrate this better, we will apply the principles of scale to something all of us can relate to: making sandwiches.

Scale in Our Day-to-Day Life

Let's take an example of scalability in action. Say it takes you a total of five minutes to pack one peanut butter and jelly sandwich for lunch, which consists of the following steps, as shown in Figure 4-1:

1. Toast two pieces of bread.
2. Spread peanut butter on one side.
3. Spread jelly on the other side.
4. Assemble the sandwich.
5. Bag the sandwich.

Figure 4-1. Steps to make a peanut butter and jelly sandwich

Simple enough and no sweat, right? Now, let's say you want to make 100 peanut butter and jelly sandwiches. The obvious next step is to invite more people to help. Now, if one sandwich takes five minutes to make, and you have a five-member team to make the 100 sandwiches, it's natural to think that it would take a total of 100 minutes to make these 100 sandwiches, assuming an equal distribution of labor and that each person makes 20 sandwiches.

In this particular example, *performance* is measured by the output in terms of unit of work done (one sandwich) and the time taken for that output (average time to make one sandwich). *Scalability* is understanding how much this average time is preserved as the unit of work done increases.

However, reality could be very different in terms of how you choose to implement this with five people. Let's take a look at two approaches:

End-to-end execution approach

In this approach, each person follows the steps to make a single sandwich, then proceeds to make the next sandwich, until they complete five sandwiches. This is illustrated in Figure 4-2.

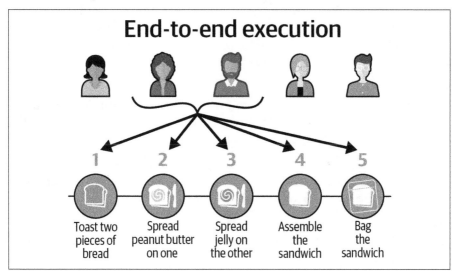

Figure 4-2. End-to-end execution

Assembly-line approach

In this approach, you have a division of labor where you distribute the steps to different people: the first person toasts the bread, the second person applies peanut butter, the third person applies the jam, and so on, as shown in Figure 4-3.

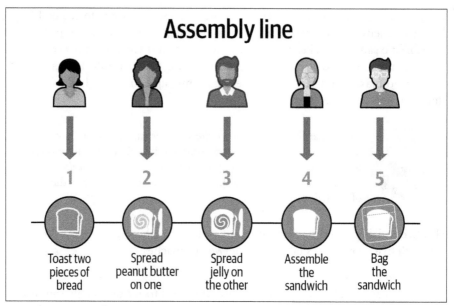

Figure 4-3. Assembly line

As you have probably guessed by now, the assembly-line approach is more efficient than the end-to-end execution approach. But what exactly makes it more efficient? To understand this, we first need to understand the fundamental concepts of what affects scaling:

Resources
> The materials that are available to make the sandwich—in this case, the bread, peanut butter, and jelly are the more obvious resources. The toaster and knives are other resources required to make the sandwich.

Task
> The set of steps that are followed to produce the output—in this case, the five steps required to make the sandwich.

Workers
> The components that perform the actual work—in this case, the people who execute the task of making the sandwich.

Output
> The outcome of the job that signals that the work is complete—in this case, the sandwich.

The *workers* utilize the *resources* to execute the *task* that produces the *output*. How effectively these come together affects the performance and scalability of the process.

Table 4-1 shows how the assembly-line approach becomes more efficient than the end-to-end execution approach.

Table 4-1. Comparison of the approaches

Area	End-to-end execution approach	Assembly-line approach
Contention for resources	All the workers end up contending for the same set of resources (toaster, jar of peanut butter, etc.).	The contention is minimal since the different workers need different resources.
Flexibility in workers to thread mapping	Low—since the workers perform all the tasks, the allocation is uniform to all tasks.	High—if some tasks need more workers than others, a quick shift is possible.
Impact of adding/ removing resources	The impact of adding resources might not make a big difference depending on which bottleneck is in the system. However, adding the right resources would speed up the execution. For example, if you have five toasters instead of one toaster, the workers can toast the bread more quickly.	The flexibility of resource allocation allows for an increase in performance when more resources are available.

Also, note that in the end-to-end execution approach, some sandwiches will take less time to complete than others. For example, when five people are reaching for the toaster and one person gets it, that particular sandwich will be done sooner than the others who have to wait for the toaster to be ready. So if you were to measure performance, you would see that the time to make a sandwich at the 50th percentile might be acceptable, but the time taken at the 75th and 99th percentiles might be a lot higher.

It would be fair to conclude that the assembly-line approach is more scalable than the end-to-end execution approach in making the sandwich. While the benefits of this scalability are not conspicuous in your normal day, such as when you may pack three or four sandwiches, the difference is really visible when the job to be done drastically increases, to making 3,000 or 4,000 sandwiches, for instance.

Scalability in Data Lake Architectures

In data lake architectures, as we saw in the previous chapters, resources are available to us from the cloud: the compute, storage, and networking resources. Additionally, there are two key factors that we own and control to best leverage the resources available to us: the processing job, which is the code we write, and the data itself, in terms of how we get to store and organize it for processing. This is illustrated in Figure 4-4.

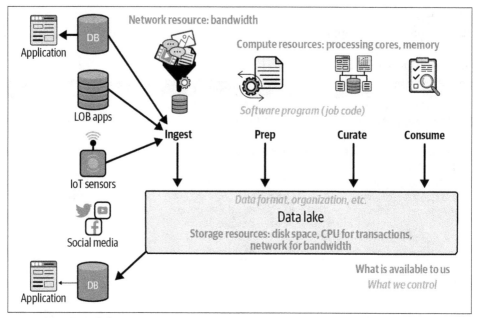

Figure 4-4. Data lake resources

They key resources available to us in a cloud data lake architecture are as follows:

Compute resource

The compute resources available to you from the cloud are primarily CPU cores and memory for your data processing needs. Additionally, there is software running on these cores, primarily the software you install in the case of IaaS and the software available to you in terms of PaaS and SaaS that is designed to manipulate and optimize the utilization of the CPU and memory resources. A key understanding of how this works is critical to building your scalable solution. Cloud service providers offer capabilities like autoscaling, where as the compute needs of your solution increases, your cloud services can automatically add more compute without you having to manage the resources. Additionally, there are serverless components like Google's BigQuery (*https://oreil.ly/6QtUO*) that completely abstract the resourcing aspects of compute and storage from the user, allowing the user to focus solely on their core business scenarios. Serverless components tend to cost more compared to tunable IaaS but offer built-in optimizations and tuning that let you focus on your core scenarios.

Networking resources

Think of your networking resource as a metaphorical cable that can send data back and forth. This is implemented on networking hardware or, in other cases, is software-defined networking.

Storage resources

Cloud data lake storage systems provide an elastic distributed storage system that gives you space to store data (in disks, flash storage, and tape drives depending on the tier of data you operate on), along with computational power to perform storage transactions and networking power to transfer data over the wire to other resources inside and outside your cloud provider.

These are the key pieces that you control:

- The code you write
- The way your data is stored and organized, which largely influences how effectively the resources are utilized
- How scalable and performant your solution is

In the next section, we'll take a deeper look at how big data processing works on a data lake architecture and the factors that affect the scalability and performance of your data lake solution.

Understanding and learning the factors that help scale the system is important for two key reasons:

- The traffic patterns on the data lake tend to be highly variable and bursty in most cases, so scaling up and down are key capabilities that need to be factored into your data lake architecture.
- Understanding the bottlenecks gives you insights into what resources need to be scaled up or down; otherwise, you run the risk of adding the wrong resources without moving the needle on the scalability of the solution.

Why Do I Need to Worry About Scalability? My Solution Runs Just Fine Today.

Speaking of 10× growth, I often see customers underestimate the value and opportunities that a data lake architecture helps unlock, and optimize their time and efforts for the short-term maxima. If you are thinking along the lines of these statements—"I just need to move my data warehouse now; I don't see any other data being important as yet," or "My first priority is to get whatever we are doing on the cloud; let me worry about the rest later," or "I have a one-year timeline to move my data to the cloud; I can't afford to think about anything else other than my current workloads"—let me assure you of a few things:

- As with any software development efforts, thinking of future scenarios helps you avoid the technical debt of having to rearchitect your solutions completely when new scenarios are enabled.

- Future-proofing your design is not as hard as you think. It's more about diligence than effort, which will set you up for success.

- According to a study published by the World Economic Forum (*https://oreil.ly/NWOqf*), digital transformation is expected to add $100 trillion to the world economy by 2025, and platform-driven interactions will drive at least two-thirds of this $100 trillion growth. It is only a matter of time before these scenarios are unlocked.

Internals of Data Lake Processing Systems

As seen in Figure 4-4, the key operations involved in big data processing are the following:

Ingest
Getting raw data from various sources into a data lake storage

Prep
Preparing the raw data to generate enriched data, by applying a schema on demand, removing or fixing erroneous data, and optimizing data formats

Curate
Generating curated data with high-value density by aggregating, filtering, and other processing of enriched data

Consume

> Consuming your data through dashboards, queries, or data-science-related explorations, to name a few, and using these insights to modify your application behavior, which falls under consumption as well

In this chapter, we'll focus on the most common use case of the big data lake, which is batch processing. In batch processing, data is ingested into the data lake in a scheduled, periodic fashion via data copies. This raw data is prepared and enriched and then further curated with ELT/ETL processing engines. Apache Spark and Apache Hadoop are the most common processing engines leveraged for the prep and curate phases. These Spark jobs run in a scheduled fashion after the ingestion or data copy is completed.

There are other use cases, such as real-time processing engines, where data is continuously ingested into the data lake and further prepared and curated. While the principles of scale that we will discuss in batch processing largely apply to real-time processing pipelines as well, there are additional constraints on the design given the continuous nature of the processing. We will not get into depth on the non-batch-processing systems in this book since the most common use cases are pertinent to batch processing. In this chapter, we also won't dive deep into the consumption use cases for BI queries and data science. There are plenty of resources available on querying patterns and data science.

We'll look at the two specific aspects of big data processing that are unique to the cloud data lake architecture:

Data copy

> This involves moving data as is from one system to another system, by, for example, ingesting data into the data lake from external sources and copying data from one storage system to another within the cloud service, such as loading data from a data lake into a data warehouse. This is the most common form of ingestion used in big data processing systems.

ETL/ELT processing

> This involves an input and output dataset, where input data is read and transformed via filtering, aggregation, and other operations to generate the output datasets. Generating data in the enriched and curated datasets falls into this category. Hadoop and Spark are the most popular processing engines, with Spark leading the area here in supporting batch, real-time, and streaming operations with the same architecture. These are the most common kinds of data prep and data curation stages of big data processing.

Data Copy Internals

There are many ways to perform data copy operations. Cloud providers and ISVs offer PaaS that copy data from one system to another in an optimized fashion. You can also leverage tools and software development kits (SDKs) to copy data, such as using the cloud provider's portal to upload or download data. In this section, we'll examine the internals of a copy job where data is read from a source and copied as such into the destination. Please note that in real life, you can also extend this simple data copy scenario to more advanced topics, such as copying a constantly changing dataset as well as cleansing datasets periodically to comply with regulatory requirements like GDPR (*https://gdpr-info.eu*). For the purposes of understanding scalability, we will focus on the simple copy process.

Components of a data copy solution

The very simplified components involved in data copy are presented in Figure 4-5.

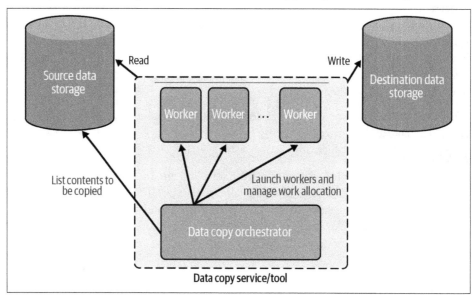

Figure 4-5. Data copy internals

The data copy tool has two main components in a simplified form:

Data copy orchestrator
> Understands the work to be done (e.g., how many files need to be copied from the source) and leverages the compute resources available to distribute the copy job across different workers. The orchestrator also preserves the state of the copy job itself, as in, it knows what data has been copied and what hasn't yet been copied.

Data copy workers
> Units of compute that accept work from the orchestrator and perform the copy operations from source to destination.

There is a configuration that specifies the number of data copy workers that you can provide to the copy job. This is a knob you can dial up or down to configure the number of workers you need, either directly by setting the maximum number of workers or by specifying a proxy value that the data copy orchestrator has defined as a configurable value.

Understanding resource utilization of a data copy job

The bottlenecks that affect the scalability and performance of your data copy are as follows:

The number and size of the files/objects that need to be copied
> The granularity of the data copy job is at the file/object level in your storage system. A large file could be chunked up to do a parallel copy, but you cannot combine multiple files into a single-copy job. If you have a lot of small files to be copied, you can expect this to take a long time because the listing operation for the operator could take longer, and the small files would make it so that in a single-copy work unit, the amount of data transferred is low, not utilizing your available bandwidth resource to the maximum possible extent.

Compute capacity of your data copy tool
> If you configure your data copy tool to have enough compute resources, then you can launch more workers, effectively making many simultaneous copy operations. On the contrary, not enough compute resources makes the number of available workers a bottleneck on your system.

Network capacity available for the copy
> The amount of networking capacity you have controls the pipe that is used for the data transfer, especially for copying data across the cloud boundary. Ensure that you have a provisioned high-bandwidth network. Please note that when you are copying or transacting between cloud services of the same provider, you don't need to provision or leverage your network; the cloud services have their own network to accomplish this.

Cross-region data copy
> When you make data copies across regions, they have to travel a longer distance over the network, which makes the data copy much slower and may even time out in some cases, causing jobs to fail.

ELT/ETL Processing Internals

If you need a refresher on how big data analytics engines work, I recommend revisiting "Big Data Analytics Engines" on page 28, specifically the section on Spark in "Apache Spark" on page 31.

ELT/ETL processes primarily work on unstructured, structured, or semistructured data, apply a schema on demand, and transform this data via filtering, aggregations, and other processing to generate structured data in a tabular format. Apache Hadoop and Apache Spark are the most common processing engines that fall in this category. We will take a deeper look at the internals of Apache Spark in this section, but the concepts largely apply to Apache Hadoop with subtle nuances. Apache Hadoop, while it can run on the cloud, was designed to run on premises on HDFS. Apache Spark is much closer to the cloud architecture. Apache Spark is also largely the de facto processing engine due to its consistency across batch, streaming, and interactive data pipelines, so we will focus on Spark in this section.

You would run an Apache Spark job in a cluster that you can create in the following ways:

- Provision IaaS compute resources and install the Apache Spark distribution either from open source Apache Spark (*https://spark.apache.org*) or from an ISV like Cloudera (*https://oreil.ly/o8NDy*).
- Provision PaaS where you can get a cluster that comes with Spark already installed and ready for you to use from vendors like Databricks (*https://oreil.ly/d3qxe*) or from cloud service providers like Amazon EMR (*https://aws.amazon.com/emr*) or Azure Synapse Analytics (*https://oreil.ly/k5nYB*).

Apache Spark leverages a distributed computing architecture, where there is a central controller/coordinator, also called the *driver*, that orchestrates the execution, and multiple *executors*, or worker units, that perform a specific task that contributes to the application. Drawing an analogy to home construction, you can think of the Apache Spark driver as the general contractor and the executors as skilled workers like plumbers and electricians. We will now go over a few key concepts that are fundamental to Apache Spark.

Components of an Apache Spark application

Data developers write Spark code and submit that code to a Spark cluster, then get results back when the execution is done. Behind the screen, the user code is executed as a *Spark application* and is divided into the following components:

Driver

The driver is the central coordinator of the Spark process and is the only component that understands the user code. The driver has two main components: define the breakdown of the jobs, tasks, and executors needed to execute the program and coordinate the assignment of these into various available parts of the Spark cluster. The cluster manager helps the driver find the resources.

Executors

The executors are the components that actually perform the computation. The driver communicates the code as well as the dataset that the executor needs to work on.

Jobs, stages, and tasks

An Apache Spark application is internally translated into an execution plan inside your Spark cluster. This execution plan is represented as a directed acyclic graph (DAG) with a set of nodes representing jobs, which in turn consist of stages that could have dependencies on one another. These stages are then broken down into tasks, which are the actual units of execution, where work is done. This is shown in Figure 4-6. The amount of executors assigned for a task depends on the amount of data that needs to be crunched.

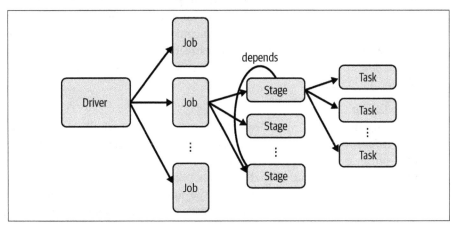

Figure 4-6. Spark job internals

Understanding resource utilization of a Spark job

As you can see, two factors contribute to the resource utilization of a Spark code:

The code

The complexity of the operations that need to be performed

The data

The volume and organization of the data that needs to be crunched

These bottlenecks affect the scalability of your data copy:

Cluster form factor and memory
> The amount of compute and memory that you provision for your Spark job heavily affects the performance of the job. When you have a compute-intensive application with a lot of data transformations, increasing the number of compute cores would provide for more executors to accomplish the tasks, resulting in overall improvement of the job. Similarly, when you have a complex transformation, if you have more memory available, the temporary datasets (RDDs) could be persisted in memory, minimizing retrieval times from slower persistent storage solutions, such as the object store. Apache Spark vendors also enable caches that help store frequently used datasets in memory.

The number and size of the files/objects that need to be operated on
> The granularity of the job execution is at the file/object level in your storage system. Similar to the data copy job, if you have a lot of small files to be read to perform your Apache Spark job, you can expect this to take a long time because the listing operation at the driver would take longer, and the overhead of reading a file (i.e., doing access checks and other metadata) has only a small return in terms of actual data read or written. On the other hand, if you crank up the number of Spark executors, you can parallelize the writes a lot faster and complete the job sooner. This is a healthy conflict because, while writes are more expensive and can be optimized by writing many small files, the subsequent reads get expensive. To minimize this downstream impact, Apache Spark provides compaction utilities that can be used to combine these small files into one large file after the job completes.

Data organization
> Processing in Apache Spark essentially involves a lot of filtering or selective data retrieval operations for reads. Organizing your data in a way that enables faster retrieval of the data in question could make a huge difference in your job performance. Columnar data formats like Parquet offer a huge benefit here; we will take a look at this in detail in the next section. In addition, effectively partitioning your data so that files/objects with similar content are organized together immensely helps optimize for quick access, requiring fewer compute resources and hence improving scalability of your solution.

Network capacity and regional boundaries
> As in the data copy scenario, the network capacity and cross-region boundaries heavily affect your performance and scalability.

A Note on Other Interactive Queries

Apache Spark is an open source technology that largely addresses batch, interactive, and real-time interactions with the data lake. Cloud data warehouses offer other interactive query technologies that are optimized for certain data formats. These formats are proprietary, and both the compute and storage systems are optimized for the formats. We are not doing a deep dive into them in this book. However, they conceptually follow the model of Spark internals at a high level.

Considerations for Scalable Data Lake Solutions

Let me start with a big disclaimer: there is no 12-step process that you can follow to the T to make your data lake performant, reliable, or scalable. However, there are several factors that contribute to the scalability and performance of your solution that you can rely on to have a robust implementation of your data lake. Think of these factors as knobs that you can tweak to understand what exactly drives your optimal performance.

If you have historical data from previous years or from your analogous on-premises implementation, you could use those as a proxy for your peak scale characteristics. However, no worries if that is not available—you could run a scaled PoC, which essentially is a copy of your workload in a simulated environment to help you understand the various factors that affect your performance, so you can see how they increase as the load on your system increases. Take your most complex job or your largest dataset to run your PoC on the data lake, and double that complexity or data size or both to analyze the impact on your resources.

In this section, we will go over some of the key factors that affect the scale and performance of your system.

Pick the Right Cloud Offerings

As we saw in the earlier sections in this chapter, you have plenty of choices of cloud offerings when it comes to your big data solutions. You can decide to compose your big data solution with IaaS, PaaS, or SaaS, either all on one cloud provider, across cloud providers (multicloud solution), or with a mix of on-premises and cloud environments (hybrid cloud solution), and in one region or multiple regions. Let's take a look at the impact of some of these choices on the overall performance and scalability of your solution.

Hybrid and multicloud solutions

Most organizations today leverage a multicloud approach, where they have invested in architectures that span two or more cloud providers. Most organizations also have hybrid cloud architectures, where they have investments across private clouds and in on-premises systems as well as with public cloud providers.

Many motivations drive a multicloud or hybrid cloud architecture:

- Migrating an on-premises platform to the cloud in phases
- Leveraging the cloud for newer scenarios and bringing back the insights to the legacy platform on premises for backward-compatibility reasons
- Minimizing vendor lock-in on a single cloud provider, the equivalent of not putting all of your eggs in one basket
- Mergers and acquisitions where different parts of the organization have their infrastructure on different clouds
- Specific requirements such as data privacy or compliance that require part of the data assets to stay on premises and not on the cloud
- Data mesh architecture, where teams or business units within the organization have the flexibility of picking the cloud providers

There are also advantages to a multicloud architecture:

- *Flexibility* of choice to the business units
- *Lower cost*—some services could be cheaper on one cloud service compared to others

However, when it comes to performance and scale, as well as the cost of the solution, there are some traps you could fall into when you have a multicloud or hybrid cloud architecture:

- *The operational cost of managing multiple clouds* could be an overhead or hidden cost that you might have overlooked. You could leverage multiple cloud management software applications, which could add to your costs.
- *Moving data out of the cloud is not optimal* in terms of performance and is also expensive. If you have a scenario where you are moving data back and forth across different cloud solutions, you would see that affecting the overall performance, and hence the scalability of the solution would be affected.
- While the fundamental concepts are similar across the services offered by different cloud providers, *deep skill sets* in terms of the nuances and best practices for

implementation are also required. Lack of these skill sets could lead to not having an optimal solution across all your environments.

- When you have scenarios where you need *low-latency, secure, direct connections to the cloud*, you need to provision specialized features like ExpressRoute from Azure (*https://oreil.ly/Pa_Ip*) or AWS Direct Connect (*https://oreil.ly/-nA8_*). You would have to provision multiple solutions to move data from your on-premises systems, thereby increasing your costs as well as your data transfers.

If you need to have a hybrid or multicloud solution, pay attention to the data transfers, and ideally ensure that the data transfers across these multiple environments are minimal and carefully thought through.

IaaS versus PaaS versus SaaS solutions

Your big data solution can be composed of a mix of IaaS, PaaS, and SaaS solutions. Here are the differences between the choices for one scenario of running a Spark notebook for your data scientists:

IaaS solution
In this solution, you would first provision virtual machine (VM) resources from the cloud provider, then install the distribution of the software—either from open source Apache Foundation or from an ISV like Cloudera—and enable the notebook access for your data scientists. You have end-to-end control of the solution; however, you also need the relevant skill sets to optimize for performance and scale. Enterprises typically follow this approach when they have engineers who can tune the open source software for their needs by building on them and when they have their custom version of the open source tools, such as Apache Hadoop or Apache Spark.

PaaS solution
In this solution, you would provision clusters from the cloud provider that offers you the right software environment (along with managing updates). You are able to specify the resources you need in terms of CPU, memory, and storage without having to understand the deep mechanics of how big data processing engines work. Most organizations follow this approach.

SaaS solution
In this solution, you would subscribe to a SaaS, such as a data warehouse and notebook service, connect them, and start using them right away. While this works great as a getting-started solution, the scalability and performance have the ceiling of the scalability of the SaaS solution itself. SaaS solutions are getting better and better, so you need to understand how much you need to scale and verify that with the SaaS provider, and confirm with a PoC as well.

Use the summary in Table 4-2 to help make the best choice.

Table 4-2. Comparison of IaaS, PaaS, and SaaS solutions

Type of service	Getting started	Flexibility to customize solution	Control over resources
IaaS	High effort: need to manage software, updates, etc.	High flexibility: you own the software stack	High control: you have control over the infrastructure-level details of the service
PaaS	High effort: lower than IaaS	Medium flexibility: as much as the PaaS service provider exposes the controls	Medium control: higher than IaaS solutions; lower than SaaS solutions
SaaS	Low effort: you can get started with your business problem almost right away	Low flexibility: ease of use comes from limited flexibility; leverage extensibility models to build on top of the SaaS	Low control: the SaaS solutions are usually multitenant (resources shared by different customers), and the resource-level details are not exposed to the customer

Cloud offerings for Klodars Corporation

Klodars Corporation planned to implement its solution as a hybrid solution, with its legacy component running on premises and its data analytics components running on the cloud. It picked PaaS for its big data cluster and data lake storage, running Apache Spark, and leveraged a SaaS solution for its data warehouse and dashboarding component. Klodars understood the impact of networking resources between its on-premises solution and its cloud provider on the performance of its solution and planned for the right capacity with the cloud provider. It also ran a PoC of the data processing workload of one of its data- and compute-intensive scenarios—product recommendation and sales projections—and ensured that it had picked a big data cluster with the right set of resources.

Klodars also segmented their clusters—one for sales scenarios, one for marketing scenarios, and one for product scenarios—to ensure that a peak workload on one did not affect the performance of the others. To promote sharing of data and insights, the data scientists had access to all of the data from product, sales, and marketing for their exploratory analysis. However, Klodars also provisioned separate clusters for the data scientists and set a limit for the resources so that there were guardrails against spurious jobs that could hog resources. You can find an overview of this implementation in Figure 4-7.

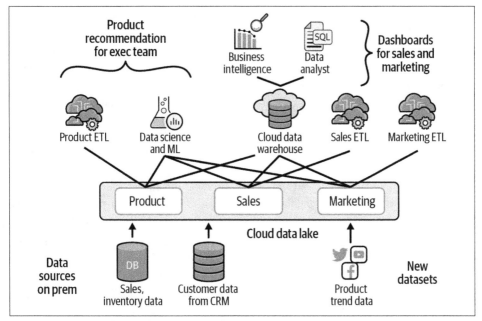

Figure 4-7. Data lake implementation at Klodars Corporation

Plan for Peak Capacity

Regardless of the type of solution you choose, planning for capacity and understanding the path to acquiring more capacity when you have additional demand are key to the cloud data lake solution. *Capacity planning* refers to the ability to predict your demand over time, ensure that you are equipped with the right resources to meet that demand, and make the right business decisions if that is not the case.

The very first step is to forecast the demand. This can be accomplished in the following ways:

- Understand your *business need and the SLAs* you need to offer to your customers. For example, if the last batch of your data arrives at 10 P.M., and your promise to your customers is that they will see a refreshed dashboard by 8 A.M., then you have a window of 10 hours to do your processing, maybe 8 hours if you would like to leave a buffer.

- Understand your *resource utilization* on the cloud. Most cloud providers offer monitoring and observability solutions that you can leverage to understand how many resources you are utilizing. For example, if you have a cluster with 4 virtual CPUs (vCPUs) and 1 GB of memory, and you observe that your workload utilizes 80% of CPU and 20% of memory overall, then you know you could go to a different SKU or cluster type that has higher CPU and lower memory, or you could take advantage of the memory to cache some results with optimizations so you can reduce the load on the CPU.

- Plan for *peak demand and peak utilization*. The big advantage of moving to the cloud is the elasticity that cloud offers. At the same time, it is always better to have a plan for exactly how you will scale your resources at peak demand. For example, your workloads today are supported by a cluster that has four vCPUs and 1 GB of memory. When you anticipate a sudden increase in load, either because it's the budget-closing season if you are running financial services or you are preparing for holiday demand if you are a retail industry, what would your plan be? Would you increase the resources on your existing clusters, or are your jobs segmented enough that you would add additional clusters on demand? If you need to bring in more data during this time from your on-premises systems, have you planned for the appropriate burst in networking capacity as well?

  You can utilize one of two scaling strategies: horizontal scaling or vertical scaling. *Horizontal scaling*, also referred to as *scaling out*, involves scoping a unit of scale (e.g., VM or cluster) and adding more of those units of scale. Your application would need to be aware of this scale unit as well. *Vertical scaling*, also referred to as *scaling up*, involves keeping the unit of scale as is and adding more resources (e.g., CPUs or memory) on demand. Either strategy works well as long as you are aware of the impact on your business need, your SLAs, and your technical implementation.

In Table 4-3, you'll see the set of factors to consider regarding monitoring and evaluating for capacity planning. Also look at the reservation models that are available, which enable critical production workloads to run without interfering with other workloads.

Table 4-3. Factors to consider for capacity planning

Component	Factors to consider
IaaS compute	vCPU (cores), memory, SKUs (type of VM), caching available, disk size (GB/TB), and transactions (TPS)
PaaS compute	Cluster size, vCPU (core) when available, and billable units published by the PaaS provider
Storage	Data size (TB/PB), transactions (TPS), and tier of storage (flash, disks, tape drives in order of high to low performance), depending on performance
Data warehouse	SKUs—watch for compute, storage, and transactions
Networking	Ingress and egress, tier (standard/premium), and gateways with private networks

To make a best guess of the capacity needs, I recommend that you run a scaled PoC that represents the workload you are running. For the PoC, you need to factor in the dataset distribution that best represents your production workload. If you are running an on-premises implementation, a great method is to run an existing workload on the cloud. If you leverage autoscaling capabilities on your cluster or serverless offerings from your cloud provider, a lot of these are automatically handled for you.

Data Formats and Job Profile

The data format you choose plays a critical role in the performance and scalability of your data lake. This is often ignored because in structured data storage systems (databases or data warehouses), this assumption was taken for granted. The data was stored in a format that was optimal for the transaction patterns of the database/data warehouse service. However, given the myriad data processing applications that run on top of the data lake storage, and the premise that the same data could be used across the multiple engines, the onus falls on the big data architects and the developers to pick the right format for their scenarios. However, the best part of this is, once you find the optimal format, you will find that your solution offers high performance and scale, along with lowered cost of your total solution. Given the rise of the data lakehouse and the ubiquity of technologies like Apache Spark for batch, streaming, and interactive computing, Apache Parquet (*https://parquet.apache.org*), and formats based on Parquet such as Delta Lake (*https://delta.io*) and Apache Iceberg (*https://iceberg.apache.org*), are being adopted widely as optimal formats for the data lake solution. We will dive deep into this in Chapter 6.

Another aspect that influences your scalability needs is the construction of your big data processing job. Typically, the job can be broken down into various stages of ingestion and processing. However, not all stages are the same. As an example, let's say that your job comprises the following steps:

1. Read a dataset that has 150 million records.
2. Filter that down to the records of interest, which are 50 million records.
3. Apply transformations on the 50 million records to generate an output dataset.

In this scenario, if your input dataset comprises multiple small files, that would serve as the long pole for your total job. By introducing a new stage in your job of compacting the multiple small files into a small number of larger files, you can make your solution more scalable.

Summary

In this section, we dove deep into the scalability characteristics of the cloud data lake architecture and how closely scalability is tied to performance. We compared a big data architecture with a disaggregated compute and storage model to a colocated tightly coupled architecture and looked at the ramifications of this disaggregation on scale. We also examined the various considerations for the cloud data lake architecture that affect the scale: picking the right cloud offerings, planning for capacity, and tuning the data formats and data organization to match the query patterns. These are considerations that you need to understand to effectively tune your data lake implementation to scale 10×. In Chapter 5, we'll build on these fundamental concepts of scale to optimize for performance.

Optimizing Cloud Data Lake Architectures for Performance

Simplicity is the ultimate sophistication.

—Leonardo da Vinci

Performance in its simplest terms can be defined as the timeliness of work completed. Having said that, this is probably one of the most loaded terms when it comes to cloud services, simply because there is no single measure for performance. In this chapter, we will peel back the layers of performance, building a good understanding of what performance means, the various dimensions associated with measuring performance when it comes to a cloud data lake, and the strategies that help optimize and tune your cloud data lake for the best performance. We will also use Klodars Corporation to illustrate these concepts and strategies.

Basics of Measuring Performance

When thinking of performance, I can say with a certain degree of confidence that you are assuming something related to speed, such as a runner crossing the finish line with a personal record. The common goal is that both strive to successfully complete their tasks and achieve a desired outcome, meeting or exceeding the spectators' expectations. In a similar vein, in a cloud data lake, performance refers to the process of setting targets for the tasks to be done and ensuring that the tasks are completed within the set targets.

The performance of a task has two aspects to it, and any measure of performance needs to incorporate these two elements:

Response time
How long did it take for the task to be completed?

Throughput
>How much output was produced?

Let's take the same example of making sandwiches that we saw in "Scale in Our Day-to-Day Life" on page 98. In that section, we saw two architectures for making sandwiches—the end-to-end execution approach shown in Figure 5-1 and the assembly line approach shown in Figure 5-2. Let's take these examples and try to measure the performance.

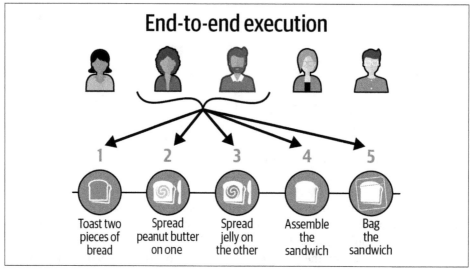

Figure 5-1. End-to-end execution approach to making sandwiches

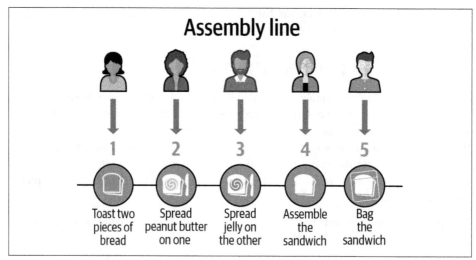

Figure 5-2. Assembly-line approach

Goals and Metrics for Performance

As I said, the performance depends on two factors: the response time and through-put. To measure performance, we need to set a goal. In the sandwich-making exam-ple, the goal is to make five sandwiches. Next, we need to identify a set of measures that are relatively easy to measure. For the purpose of simplicity, we will assume that all the workers have the same speed when making sandwiches, and there is no transition time between tasks. We will consider variable and constant measures:

Variable measures

The following measures are variables—that is, the things you can tune or change by adding or removing:

- Number of workers = five

- Number of toasters = one toaster with space for four pieces of bread

- Number of jars of peanut butter = one

- Number of jars of jelly = one

- Number of bags of bread = one

- Number of bags = five (for the number of sandwiches needed)

Constant measures

These are measures that stay relatively constant as you change the variable measures. In this example, the variable measure is the time it takes for each step to be completed:

- Step 1, toast the bread: 30 seconds

- Step 2, smear peanut butter for one sandwich: 5 seconds

- Step 3, smear jelly for 1 sandwich: 5 seconds

- Step 4, put them together: 1 second

- Step 5, bag them: 4 seconds

Given that there are limited resources, there will be scenarios where one person will need to wait for the resources to be freed before performing their task, so you will find that each of the five sandwiches will be completed at different times.

Now, are you wondering if the pages from a cookbook have been accidentally added to this book? If yes, fear not. In a cloud data lake architecture, there are components of storage, networking, and compute that are similar to the toasters or the jars of peanut butter, and they take a certain amount of time to perform an action, which contributes to your big data processing scenarios. By both optimizing the time taken to perform the action and controlling the units of these components, you can opti-mize the cloud data lake performance overall. My goal for explaining these concepts in the context of sandwich making is to make them easy to visualize and then apply in the context of cloud data lake architectures.

Measuring Performance

Let's now apply the variables we've defined to understand how much time it takes to complete making the sandwiches.

In the end-to-end execution method, one person does all the tasks required in sequential order to make the sandwich. Let's break down how the sandwich making will work. Person 1 and Person 2 will be able to use the toaster from the time our metaphorical stopwatch begins at zero, but the others have to wait for the toaster. Similarly, after the toasting is done, Person 1 will proceed to spread peanut butter from the jar, but Person 2 must wait for them to finish, and so on.

Let's say that everyone starts at Time 00:00 (minute and second, pick the hour of your choice). Table 5-1 shows the time taken to complete the sandwiches.

Table 5-1. Time taken to make the sandwiches in the end-to-end execution approach

Sandwich	Step 1	Step 2	Step 3	Step 4	Step 5	Total time taken since 00:00
1	00:00–00:30	00:30–00:35	00:35–00:40	00:40–00:41	00:41–00:45	45 seconds
2	00:00–00:30	00:35–00:40	00:40–00:45	00:45–00:46	00:46–00:50	50 seconds
3	00:30–01:00	01:00–01:05	01:05–01:10	01:10–01:11	01:11–01:15	75 seconds
4	00:30–01:00	01:05–01:10	01:10–01:15	01:15–01:16	01:16–01:20	80 seconds
5	01:00–01:30	01:30–01:35	01:35–01:40	01:40–01:41	01:41–01:45	105 seconds

In the assembly-line method, we already see that a different model is in place and the time taken would be different, where each person does exactly one task and then hands over the sandwich to the next person, forming an assembly line. In this case, when the first person toasts the bread for two sandwiches, they move on to toast the next set of bread slices, while the bread for the first two sandwiches is passed off to the second and third people, who smear the peanut butter and jelly, respectively, at the same time. Table 5-2 shows how this model affects the performance.

Table 5-2. Time taken to make the sandwiches in the assembly-line approach

Sandwich	Step 1	Step 2	Step 3	Step 4	Step 5	Total time taken since 00:00
1	00:00–00:30	00:30–00:35	00:35–00:40	00:40–00:41	00:41–00:45	45 seconds
2	00:00–00:30	00:35–00:40	00:40–00:45	00:41–00:42	00:42–00:46	46 seconds
3	00:30–01:00	01:00–01:05	01:05–01:10	01:10–01:11	01:11–01:15	75 seconds
4	00:30–01:00	01:05–01:10	01:10–01:15	01:11–01:12	01:12–01:16	76 seconds
5	01:00–01:30	01:30–01:35	01:35–01:40	01:40–01:41	01:41–01:45	105 seconds

As I mentioned earlier, performance is not a singular measure. In this setup, the time taken to make all the sandwiches is 105 seconds in both cases. However, to measure the performance characteristics, we need to look at what the 60th and 80th percentiles of time were. To measure this, we essentially have an ordered list of all the times from smallest to biggest value, and find the value under which 60% and 80% of the values fall.

In this case, the 60th percentile for both architectures is 75 seconds; however, the 80th percentile is 80 seconds in the end-to-end execution approach versus 76 seconds in the assembly-line approach.

In cloud data lake architectures, the task is similar to sandwich making, where performance is not measured for a single unit of work, also known as a *job*, but in terms of percentiles where multiple jobs are running at the same time, and what is the average time for job completion (50th percentile) versus the worst-case times (75th or 90th percentiles). The reason is that in real life, the cloud data lake is running multiple jobs at scale. In the example of a copy job, the logical job consists of copying hundreds or thousands of files, which are multiple copy jobs, and the time taken for copying files depends on when the resources are available, similar to the sandwiches waiting for the toaster.

Optimizing for Faster Performance

From Table 5-1 and Table 5-2, we observe the following:

- The largest bottleneck happens in the toaster, where it takes 30 seconds to toast the sandwich.
- The people performing Step 2, Step 3, Step 4, and Step 5 have periods of waiting, idle time. Their idle time is more than their work time, in fact.
- The assembly-line approach and the end-to-end approach are quite similar, but the assembly-line approach has a slight edge by optimizing the time of the person who is putting the pieces of bread together.
- Steps 4 and 5 don't have any contention for shared resources. This is because Step 4 does not require any resources and Step 5 has enough resources to not be shared.

To optimize performance, there are many possible options:

- You can increase resources—you can get two toasters, two jars of peanut butter, and two jars of jelly.
- In the assembly-line approach, you can allocate workers differently. You can add two more workers for a total of six workers, and you can have two workers each do Step 2 (spread peanut butter) and Step 3 (spread jelly), and two workers do

both Step 4 (put the pieces of bread together) and Step 5 (bag the sandwich). The end-to-end execution approach does not offer this flexibility.

With these changes, let's see how the performance of the two architectures changes, as shown in Table 5-3 and Table 5-4.

Table 5-3. Time taken to make the sandwiches in the end-to-end execution approach after adding resources and shifting workers

Sandwich	Step 1	Step 2	Step 3	Step 4	Step 5	Total time taken since 00:00
1	00:00–00:30	00:30–00:35	00:35–00:40	00:40–00:41	00:41–00:45	45 seconds
2	00:00–00:30	00:30–00:35	00:35–00:40	00:40–00:41	00:41–00:45	45 seconds
3	00:00–00:30	00:35–00:40	00:40–00:45	00:45–00:46	00:46–00:50	50 seconds
4	00:00–00:30	00:35–00:40	00:40–00:45	00:45–00:46	00:46–00:50	50 seconds
5	00:30–01:00	01:00–01:05	01:05–01:10	01:10–01:11	01:11–01:15	75 seconds

In the assembly-line method, we already see that there is a different model in place, and the time taken is different.

Table 5-4. Time taken to make the sandwiches in the assembly-line approach after adding resources and shifting workers

Sandwich	Step 1	Step 2	Step 3	Steps 4 and 5	Total time taken since 00:00
1	00:00–00:30	00:30–00:35	00:35–00:40	00:40–00:45	45 seconds
2	00:00–00:30	00:30–00:35	00:35–00:40	00:40–00:45	45 seconds
3	00:00–00:30	00:35–00:40	00:40–00:45	00:45–00:50	50 seconds
4	00:00–00:30	00:35–00:40	00:40–00:45	00:45–00:50	50 seconds
5	00:30–01:00	01:00–01:05	01:05–01:10	01:10–01:15	75 seconds

With the tuning, we were able to bring the total time taken to make the sandwiches down to 75 seconds in both the architectures, and the 60th and 80th percentiles dropped to 50 seconds. Although both architectures show similar results, it's clear that the assembly-line approach is a lot more flexible in terms of tuning compared to the end-to-end execution approach, where the only way to improve performance is to add resources. Adding workers would have no effect, and shifting workers around is not possible.

Typically, this is how performance is measured, only instead of five sandwiches, think of millions or billions of operations on a cloud data lake. The 50th percentile is a proxy of the average behavior, the 75th percentile is a good proxy for perceived behavior that you want to set targets for, and the 90th percentile is a good measure of behavior under heavy load. Now that we understand these concepts, let's take a look at how they relate to the cloud data lake.

Cloud Data Lake Performance

In the world of data lakes, performance is measured by the time it takes to complete a job, whether it is a batch pipeline, an interactive query, or a data copy job, and how this time increases as the throughput of the job—the data to be crunched or queried—changes. As we saw in the sandwich-making example, performance is very tuned to the kind of job we are doing and the business requirements we need to meet. In the sandwich-making example, if a caterer has an order to be delivered by 8 A.M., that is the target set for them. They typically wouldn't have infinite time for this either, because the sandwiches need to taste fresh. So in this case, they would tune the available workers (the sandwich makers) and the resources (jars of peanut butter and jelly, toasters) to fit the time window they have. Although it costs the caterers more to pay for these resources and workers, not investing in them or not utilizing them the right way risks their order delivery, thereby risking their customer satisfaction and revenue. On the other hand, if it were a retailer making clothes, in addition to the workers and the resources, they can play with the time factor to build an inventory that has reserves of clothes made ahead of time.

Similarly, the first step to architecting a performant data lake is to understand the jobs to be done and the requirements that the jobs need to meet.

SLAs, SLOs, and SLIs

To define the requirements for performance, there are three terms you need to understand:

Service-level agreements
> SLAs refer to the promise we make to our customers as a guarantee. This SLA could be measured in terms of timing, freshness of the data, or other factors, or a combination of multiple metrics. This metric is measured in a customer-oriented language. For example, sales projection data up until 9 P.M. the day before will be available in the data warehouse for business analysts by 10 A.M. any given day, 99% of the time. SLAs serve as a contract between the service provider and the customer, and not meeting the SLA has consequences, in terms of escalations or even monetary impacts.

Service-level objectives
> SLOs are defined for each block of the solution, and they are goals that need to be met to be able to fulfill the SLAs. This metric is measured at a system level and is derived from the customer-level metrics. For example, if the sales projection data needs to be ready at 10 A.M. in the warehouse, then the Spark job that processes this data needs to be ready at least by 8 A.M. to account for buffers. If the input data for the Spark job is only available at 5 A.M., then the SLO for that Spark job

is that it needs to complete within three hours. If the SLOs are not met, then the SLAs are potentially threatened, and the team has to take action.

Service-level indicators

SLIs are also defined for each block of the solution and drill down to deeper levels in the individual components of the block. They are measures of how the system is actually doing. For example, the SLIs for this Spark job will be metrics on the performance of the executors and the driver at the 50th, 75th, and 90th percentiles as well as measures of CPU, memory, storage, and network usage of the jobs. The SLIs serve as indicators for the SLOs and alert the team to investigate risks.

Example: How Klodars Corporation Managed Its SLAs, SLOs, and SLIs

To illustrate these concepts, let's make a trip to our fictitious Klodars Corporation and take a look at their sales team requirements. Klodars Corporation has a daily executive briefing at 9 A.M. where they look at the daily sales data for their products; this data helps the team strategize about the plans and allocations for the day and is time used for inventory planning. This requirement defines the needs for the SLA. The sales team and the data team agree on a contract that the sales dashboards will be refreshed with the new data by 9 A.M. This becomes the SLA that the data team promises the sales team.

The data team then works backward from this SLA and defines the requirements for their copy jobs and Spark jobs. The data team knows that the latest data lands in their sales databases by 3 A.M., and a dump of that data needs to be copied over to the data lake storage to serve as input for the Spark jobs. The Spark jobs crunch the data from this sales database with other data to produce the datasets that power the sales dashboard. This understanding helps the data team set goals for their copy job and Spark job appropriately. The Spark job needs to be completed by 8 A.M. to give a one-hour buffer for any unforeseen issues. So the data team has a window between 3 A.M. and 8 A.M. to meet its SLAs. The team runs a few PoCs and defines the goals as three hours or less for the copy job and two hours or less for the Spark job. These become the SLOs.

The team then builds metrics dashboards about the copy job progress tracking as well as the Spark job progress tracking, along with the finer granular details pertaining to both jobs. These metrics serve as the SLIs. These concepts are illustrated in Figure 5-3.

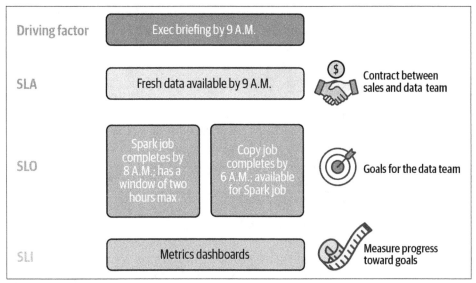

Figure 5-3. Klodars Corporation working on SLAs, SLOs, and SLIs

A pictorial representation of how these metrics align with the architecture of Klodars Corporation is shown in Figure 5-4.

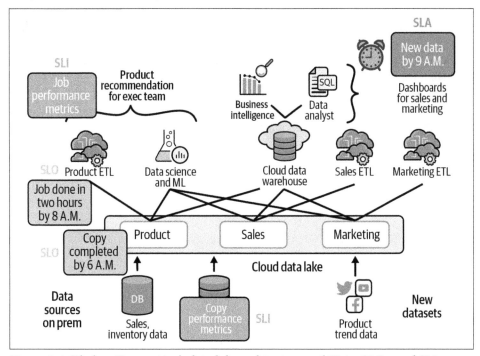

Figure 5-4. Klodars Corporation's data lake architecture and SLAs, SLOs, and SLIs

These become the defining requirements for deciding what kind of architecture and technical components serve as the best choices to meet the SLAs while optimizing for cost and operational burden on the data team.

Drivers of Performance

In "Internals of Data Lake Processing Systems" on page 104, we learned how big data processing engines work internally, specifically for data copy jobs and ELT/ETL processing jobs. In this section, we'll build on those concepts to understand the drivers of performance in each scenario.

Performance Drivers for a Copy Job

The copy job primarily reads contents from a source storage system and copies them over to a destination source system. Performance drivers of the copy job are essentially the workers and shared resources that create a potential bottleneck, depending on the type and amount of contents to be copied. For example, if there are a large number of small objects, then you could increase the number of workers to read the individual objects more quickly, resulting in an overall optimization in job performance. However, if you don't have enough network bandwidth, then these workers will be waiting for bandwidth to be available before they can read the files and copy, so the workers might stay idle, just like we saw in our sandwich-making example in "Basics of Measuring Performance" on page 119, where the workers had to wait for the toaster to be available. A representation of these performance drivers as they align to the copy job internals is shown in Figure 5-5. These are the variables you can modify to tune the performance of your copy job.

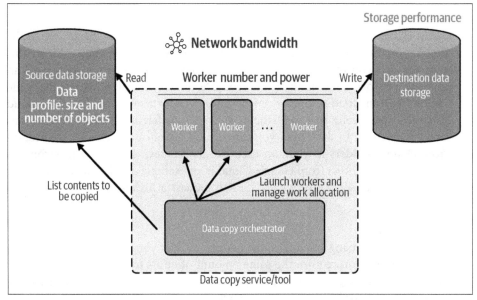

Figure 5-5. Performance drivers for copy job

The copy jobs are performed by ingestion services that are provided by public cloud providers, such as Azure Data Factory (*https://oreil.ly/bcsK3*), AWS Data Pipeline (*https://oreil.ly/6wbsK*), or AWS Glue (*https://aws.amazon.com/glue*). AWS Glue and Azure Data Factory offer integrations with ELT processing in addition to data copy. The copy jobs are also offered by various ISVs providing data integration capabilities, such as Fivetran, WANdisco, and Stitch. You can also orchestrate data copy jobs by provisioning IaaS VMs and running your software, such as Apache Airflow (*https:// airflow.apache.org*), to write your own data movement jobs. To optimize the copy job for better performance, the different knobs you can tweak are as follows:

Number of workers and power of workers
> PaaS solutions offer packaged units of work that you can increase or decrease to improve the performance of the jobs. As an example, Azure Data Factory offers this as Data Integration Units, or DIUs (*https://oreil.ly/wn83t*). If you are using IaaS or VMs, you will be able to tune the configuration of the VMs that control the amount of CPU and memory available to you as well as leverage your data copy job configurations around parallel units, which let you configure the number of workers that can run in parallel.

Network bandwidth

Network bandwidth can be compared to a pipe that connects the source to the destination, and by increasing bandwidth, you can increase the width of this pipe that lets you transfer more data in parallel. There are many ways you can increase network bandwidth. When you are transferring data within the same region between cloud resources, this is automatically taken care of by your cloud provider. Specifically in cases where you are transferring data from your on-premises systems to the cloud, you can request a dedicated network connection from cloud providers to your on-premises datacenters. Dedicated Interconnect (*https://oreil.ly/OjA0c*) from Google Cloud is an example of this. You can also talk to your internet service provider (ISP) to request a higher-bandwidth network connection.

Data size and formats

When you have many small files, the performance of your data copy job will dip. This is because you require the same amount of effort to set up the connection and do the data copy preparation, which is a fixed cost that is a sunken cost or an overhead. And the amount of data actually copied is lower compared to this overhead, giving you a lower return on investment. A worthy step is to compact multiple smaller files into a larger file in your source before copying it into your cloud data lake. Similarly, optimizing your files in a storage-friendly format like Apache Parquet helps in this case.

Performance Drivers for a Spark Job

Spark jobs have a lot more nuanced details that affect the job performance, and there are a lot of optimizations built as tunable parameters in your Spark cluster. From a conceptual point of view, the performance drivers of a Spark job can be summarized into four categories, and there are specific parameters that can be tuned within each category.

Figure 5-6 depicts the performance drivers as they relate to the Spark job internals.

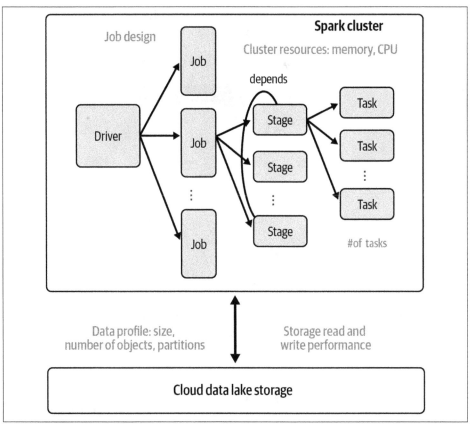

Figure 5-6. Performance drivers of a Spark job

There are four different classes of parameters that control the performance of the Spark job:

Spark cluster configurations

This class of configurations corresponds to the amount of resources, in terms of memory and CPU, that are allocated to the PaaS or IaaS where you run Spark. PaaS will expose this configuration in terms of the resources you can allocate to the drivers and the worker nodes. As a reminder, the driver is the primary orchestrator of the Spark job that determines how the data is distributed to the workers, and the workers perform the actual computations—that is, actually execute the Spark job on a sliver of the dataset that is assigned to them. As an example, Figure 5-7 is a screenshot showing how you configure a Databricks cluster on AWS, as seen on the Databricks documentation page (*https://oreil.ly/ XJUUF*). You will be able to allocate the flavor of the Elastic Compute Cloud (EC2) VM to the driver node and the number and flavor of EC2 VMs that you allocate to the worker nodes. This also displays right alongside the number of cores (that is a proxy of CPU) and the amount of memory available in your cluster. Databricks also offers an autoscaling service, which automatically scales the compute resources up or down depending on the demands of the job.

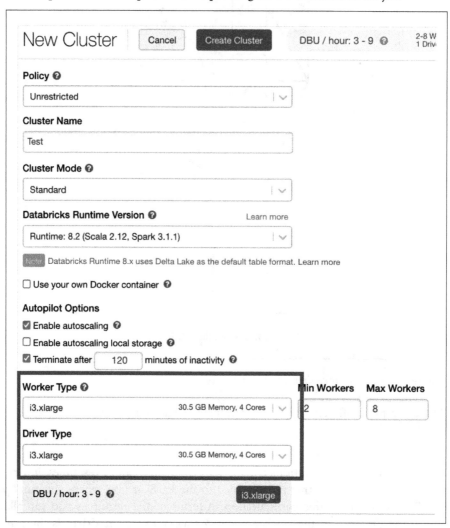

Figure 5-7. Databricks cluster configurations on AWS

If you are running Spark on IaaS VMs, you will manage the flavor and number of VMs yourself. The question that you would ask at this point is how to determine the amount of resources you need. While you can use existing best practice articles as a starting point, in my opinion, a PoC, running a scaled-down version of your job and studying the characteristics of the resource consumption, is the most accurate way to understand what your job demands.

Spark job configurations

The Spark job configurations essentially help you tune how the Spark job is broken down into executable chunks and how the chunks are effectively leveraging the available resources. To better understand these, I will walk through the internals of how a Spark job is executed and explain these parameters in context in "Choosing the Right Configurations on Apache Spark" on page 142.

Data lake storage performance: input/output operations per second (IOPS), throughput, contention with other jobs

The least talked about resource in a data lake architecture when it comes to performance is the data lake storage. Although the data lake storage offers elastic scale and there is nothing specific to configure here, what matters is that the storage is a shared resource across multiple compute engines that could be running on the data lake storage. *IOPS* refers to the number of storage transactions (reads, writes, or metadata operations such as list) it can support per second. *Throughput* refers to the amount of data that can be input or output per second. If your Spark job and another job are contending with the same dataset or competing for the same shared storage resources, such as the AWS S3 bucket or the Azure storage account, then both these jobs are contending for the same data access, creating a bottleneck. One way for you to work with this problem is to ensure that you orchestrate your jobs carefully to avoid this bottleneck.

Data profile: the number of objects, size of the data, partitioning, and formats

Data formats play a critical role in job performance, and this is possibly the first place that you can optimize in your data lake architecture. This is an area your data platform team has complete control over, and optimizing your data not only improves your job performance but also reduces the overall cost of your solution, because you end up needing much fewer resources. In "Data Formats" on page 134, I will dive into data formats in deeper detail.

 A Note on Network Bandwidth for Spark Jobs

You may have noticed that we have not called out network bandwidth as a constraint for Spark jobs. The reason is that when you design your Spark jobs, you need to ensure that the compute is as close to storage as possible. If you have scenarios such as cross-region data access, network bandwidth would definitely be a constraint.

Optimization Principles and Techniques for Performance Tuning

There are a few key principles that tune your job performance:

Plan for enough resources
Ensure there are enough compute, storage, and network resources available for your job. Provision the right amount and configuration of these resources, and make sure that noncritical jobs don't contend with your critical jobs for the same resources, as we saw in "Performance Drivers for a Spark Job" on page 130. If you need a more detailed refresher, we covered this in "Pick the Right Cloud Offerings" on page 111 and "Plan for Peak Capacity" on page 115.

Leverage best practices for optimal data access
With your data formats, data organization with partitioning, and job profiles across the board, you need to ensure that you access only the data that you want. If you end up reading more and then filtering, you are not optimizing your resource usage.

Take time to find the right configurations
All big data compute engines provide out-of-the-box configurations that can be fine-tuned based on your needs. Having the right configurations ensures that the right amount of resources are utilized in executing your jobs. Depending on the services that you pick, work with these configurations and understand better how they apply to your job. This information is very pertinent to the technology and the provider you pick.

Let's take a look at data formats and the right configurations in more detail.

Data Formats

As we saw before, data lake architecture supports many compute engines on top of the same data. However, the data format optimizations are based on a few key assumptions:

- Data stored in a data lake that is actively transacted is largely in a tabular format (organized as rows and columns).

- Data that is written once is read multiple times.

- The read patterns largely rely on conditional selection of data, where data that has similar values for certain columns is filtered to be returned or aggregated to be grouped.

A format that has gained wide industry adoption is Apache Parquet. We'll take a deeper look at Apache Parquet next.

Exploring Apache Parquet

Apache Parquet is a column-oriented data format used to store tabular data: data in the form of a table with rows and columns. Apache Parquet essentially splits a table into smaller chunks, where data is stored in a column-oriented format. To illustrate this better, as shown in Figure 5-8, there is a table with four rows. A single row is referred to as a *record* within the table. In a row-optimized format, such as a CSV file, data for a record is stored together. However, in a column-optimized format like Apache Parquet, the data of a column is encoded and stored together.

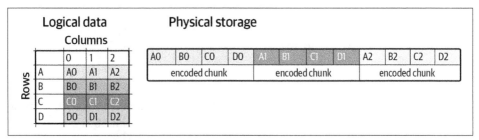

Figure 5-8. Column chunking in Apache Parquet

There are a couple of advantages to this approach:

- The storage format is optimized for reads because you don't waste resources seeking and reading columns that you don't need in the query.
- Given that the data in a column is similar, it can be packed together, offering better compression. This better compression results in lower costs for both storage and transactions.

In addition, Apache Parquet offers the following advantages:

- Parquet offers a high degree of compression with its format options. It also offers options for users to pick a compression option, such as Gzip or Snappy, and lets users choose the data encoding.
- The columnar format of Parquet lends itself to modern CPU architectures, better leveraging their native instruction set formats and offering better performance.

When it comes to storing data in Apache Parquet format, remember that we're talking about tables that have hundreds of millions of rows. Storing all of them in a single file is not going to be optimal because it will cause bottlenecks in both reads and writes doing single-file operations.

Let's now take a look at how data is structured within the Parquet file. At a high level, a single table in Apache Parquet is stored across multiple files in your storage system. Here are the concepts you need to be familiar with when it comes to Apache Parquet:

Block

Block refers to the physical representation of data within a Parquet file. The block size is 128 MB by default and can be configured in the block size parameter that is associated with a table.

Row group

This is the logical representation of a partition of data within the table as well as the minimum amount of data that can be read from a Parquet file.

Column chunk

The chunk within the row group is where data for a single column across the records in the row group is stored together. Data within the chunk is stored continuously.

Data page

The data pages are contained within the column chunk and contain the actual data for that column. A page is the basic indivisible unit within the Parquet file.

Metadata

Every Parquet file has a header and a footer. The footer contains metadata about the records within the row, including the number of records contained in the row group, the type of encoding used, the schema of the data, and the unique range of values of columns within the Parquet file. When a Parquet file is read, the footer is read first to understand if the range of the values of columns in the Parquet file has data that matches the selection criteria in the query, and if not, the pages are skipped, optimizing to read only the data that you want.

Figure 5-9 walks through the layout of the row groups, column chunks, and data pages in a Parquet file, referenced in the Apache Parquet documentation (*https://oreil.ly/MQvuj*).

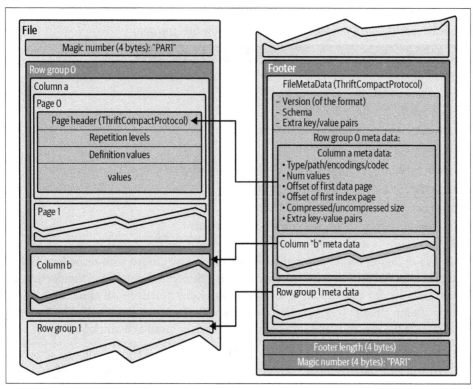

Figure 5-9. Apache Parquet data format (adapted from Apache Parquet (https://oreil.ly/MQvuj))

Let's take a look at how Apache Parquet helps with optimization for reads. Reads in a big data processing system often query for specific columns within a table and have a selection criteria to return only the records that meet specific conditions. If you are already familiar with SQL, this is similar to a SELECT statement. If not, we'll take a quick detour to walk through an example.

Let's walk through one of the datasets that the New York City Taxi and Limousine Commission (*https://oreil.ly/yClYU*) publishes for taxi data. In fact, if you are looking for datasets to practice your big data processing skills on, this is a great dataset to start with. One of the datasets contains the records corresponding to trips by Yellow cabs. There are a total of 17 fields in this dataset; refer to the data dictionary (*https://oreil.ly/69nE3*) for the complete set of fields. We will look at a subset of fields for this example (Table 5-5).

Table 5-5. Select fields from the New York City Yellow taxi trip data

Field	Description
VendorID	The provider who shared this data
tpep_pickup_datetime	Time when meter was engaged
tpep_dropoff_datetime	Time when meter was disengaged
passenger_count	Number of passengers
trip_distance	Distance traveled
payment_type	Type of payment (including disputed/voided payments)
fare_amount	Fare charged by the meter
tip_amount	Tips for credit card payments
total_amount	Total amount including fare, tip, and taxes

This data in Parquet will be stored where there are row groups with records of Yellow taxi data trips. Within the row groups, there is one column chunk for VendorID, one column chunk for pick-up time, one column chunk for drop-off time, and so on. These column chunks will contain data pages with the actual data itself. The footer of this Parquet file will contain ranges of data for each column as a quick lookup.

Let's say you're querying what the fare and tips were for all trips made on January 5, 2022. It will look like Example 5-1. Perform the following operations logically:

1. Filter for transactions that were performed on January 5, 2022.

2. Select the fare amount and tip amount and total them.

Example 5-1. Pseudocode for the query of fare and tips made from all trips on January 5, 2022

```
select (sum of fare_amount) and (sum of tip_amount)
from yellow_taxi_trip_table
where
tpep_pickup_datetime is between 12 AM and 11:59 PM on January 5, 2022 and
tpep_dropoff_datetime is between 12 AM and 11:59 PM on January 5, 2022
```

If this query were to be done in a CSV file, all records would need to be loaded from storage into compute, and the filtering and the aggregation would happen inside the compute. However, queries on an Apache Parquet file happen as follows:

1. Read the footer of the Parquet file to find where the row groups and column chunks are within that file, and check the column ranges for tpep_pickup_date time and tpep_dropoff_datetime. Skip the row groups where the date ranges of the pick-up and drop-off columns are outside the range of January 5, 2022.

2. For the row groups where the date ranges match, only read the columns corresponding to `fare_amount` and `tip_amount`, and return them to the compute engine for aggregation. The rest of the columns can be skipped.

In a table with 17 columns and millions of rows, you are effectively reading only two columns corresponding to a subset of the records and skipping the rest. This by itself offers huge optimizations by minimizing the compute needs required for the filtering as well as minimizing the storage reads.

Apache Parquet provides configurable parameters for block size and row group size that you can use to optimize for performance based on your query patterns. It is a best practice to keep your block size and row group size as close as possible.

For deeper exploration, a lot of resources and blogs are available on Apache Parquet. The Apache Parquet documentation (*https://oreil.ly/ncveb*) does a great job walking through the details. I highly recommend you read this closely since it builds a solid foundation for understanding the basics of analytics data processing. There are a lot of videos and tutorials discussing Parquet and its application in analytics in great depth that I recommend you check out for a deeper understanding. One such video is the talk at the Spark+AI Summit 2019 by Boudewijn Braams titled "The Parquet Format and Performance Optimization Opportunities." (*https://oreil.ly/wkUep*) There are also statistics such as the ones published by Databricks (*https://oreil.ly/EjvMb*) on how Parquet offers lower costs with smaller data size as well as performance with query runtimes.

Other popular data formats

Various other data formats that are built on top of Apache Parquet have gained popularity, including Delta Lake (*https://delta.io*), Apache Iceberg (*https://iceberg.apache.org*), and Apache Hudi (*https://hudi.apache.org*). They all build on the Apache Parquet architecture and are optimized for specific scenarios. Delta Lake was designed to support the data lakehouse architecture, supporting SQL-like queries for BI scenarios on the data lake. Apache Iceberg was founded to overcome the inherent disadvantages of the append-only architecture of cloud object storage systems to provide better change management for datasets. Apache Hudi was incubated by Uber to support streaming data scenarios with incremental data pipelines. We will look more closely at these formats in Chapter 6.

How Klodars Corporation picked their data formats

Alice and her team understood the importance of data formats in their organization and ensured that their data preparation jobs stored the enriched and curated data in Apache Parquet. Based on analyzing their use cases, the time values (e.g., dates of sales, inventory dates) and regional information were most commonly used for queries and dashboards, so they optimized their Parquet files in a way that they were organized based on the dates and regions. This greatly improved the query performance for their dashboards, and their business analysts were more productive. Since the format offered a very high degree of compression, they were able to demonstrate savings in data storage costs that were well appreciated by the finance teams and executive leadership. Alice and her team are also evaluating the use of Delta Lake or Apache Iceberg as the first step to running the data lakehouse pattern they are going to explore.

Data Organization and Partitioning

In the previous section, we saw how important the data formats are, as they are in effect how data is organized inside a file. In addition, when loading data into the data lake or writing data with big data processing tools, it's important to understand how to organize the data storage itself. For example, think of organizing your closet, where you have one section for activewear, another for special occasions, and another for work clothes. Within those sections, you organize even further, such as sorting your summer wear and winter wear separately. Similarly, provisioning sections of your data lake to store data and how to organize the data storage within those sections is what we will focus on.

Why is this data organization important? Two factors contribute to this:

- Reading an object or reading a file involves two operations:

    Metadata operations
    Finding the file within the storage by listing the contents, making the access checks to ensure that the caller has access to the file/object, checking the integrity of the file/object, and so forth. While metadata operations are very important, these are more like overheads to get to the actual data.

    Data operations
    Actually working with the contents of the file/object—the read and write operations. These are the high-value operations that are relevant to the business aspect.

- Data transfer from storage to compute involves data transfer over the network.

Let's now put into perspective how this affects performance and scale.

Metadata operations are an overhead to get to the actual data operations. So in your big data processing, you need to ensure that you minimize the metadata operations compared to the data read/written. Consider the following scenarios that illustrate how larger file sizes make for efficient read operations, minimizing the metadata overhead:

One hundred objects, each 1 MB in size
> To read 100 MB of data, you need to perform metadata operations on 100 objects.

Ten objects, 10 MB in size
> To read 100 MB of data, you need to perform metadata operations on 10 objects.

One object, 100 MB in size
> To read 100 MB of data, you need to perform metadata operations on one object.

Most read operations involve conditionally selective queries. You have multiple options to accomplish this, and each involves sending data between storage and compute over the wire. As you can see, improvements in selections of the data minimize the data transferred over the wire:

- Read 500 MB of data from storage into compute, and perform the filtering in the compute engine to select the relevant 100 MB: this is inefficient because you are sending more data over the wire, and you are spending additional compute to do the filtering.

- Organize the 500 MB efficiently, so you can find the 100 MB you need with that organization and send it over the wire: this is a more efficient approach.

Data partitioning is the process of effectively organizing data in your objects in a way that makes retrieval easy. Whether the organization is based on AWS or GCP buckets or Azure folders and containers, you are optimizing it for retrieval. In a tabular data structure, partitions are typically based on columns that are most the commonly queried.

Optimal data organization strategy for Klodars Corporation

Alice and her team wanted to explore various ways to partition their data. They took a closer look at their sales data, which most of their customers queried on, and brainstormed various options to organize it, as shown in Figure 5-10:

- *Option 1*: Organize data by regions followed by salesperson; this option is optimized for queries where regional sales patterns are most commonly used, followed by individual performance.

- *Option 2*: Organize data by time, followed by regions; this option is optimized for queries where trend over time is most commonly used, followed by regional pivots.

- *Option 3*: Organize data by regions, followed by time; this option is optimized for queries where regional sales patterns are most commonly used, followed by trends over time.

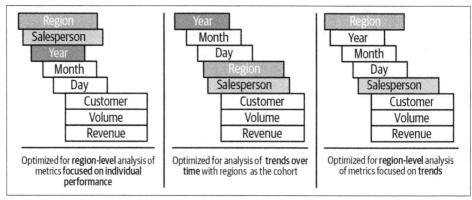

Figure 5-10. Data-partitioning options at Klodars Corporation

They interviewed the consumers and looked at the query trends on the data lake and data warehouse. They determined that the most common query pattern was regional, followed by trends over time, so they chose Option 2 as their partitioning strategy. They repeated this analysis for their other datasets and ensured that the partitioning strategy met their usage patterns.

Choosing the Right Configurations on Apache Spark

I talked about the internals of Apache Spark in "Components of an Apache Spark application" on page 108. As a quick recap, the Spark application has the code for a Spark job, and a job is broken down into stages, which are further broken down into tasks that are units of execution, as shown in Figure 5-11. There are two units of compute: the driver that orchestrates the job execution by assigning datasets to workers and the workers that do the actual execution of a part of the job. The data is persisted in memory datasets called RDDs that the executors operate on.

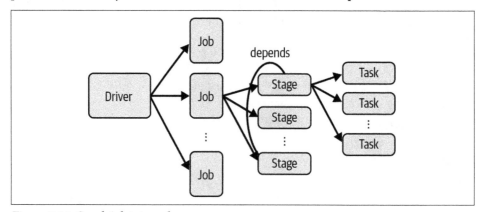

Figure 5-11. Spark job internals

Apache Spark provides configurable parameters that can be tuned so that the job is executed with optimal resource utilization in terms of CPU and memory. This process of setting the right parameters for effective utilization of CPU and memory is called *performance tuning*. The tunable parameters of Apache Spark fall into the following categories:

Data serialization

Apache Spark offers libraries that serialize the datasets—that is, convert logical objects into a series of bytes to be sent over the network or persist in disk storage in an efficient fashion. When you write your core Spark applications, you write code to transform the data via filtering, aggregation, joins, and so on. This dataset, whether it is the input or the transformed dataset, is serialized before it is sent to the executors, as shown in Figure 5-12. Apache Spark offers serialization in Java as well as in Kryo (*https://oreil.ly/MYLMm*) libraries, which offer faster, more efficient serialization compared to Java. Leveraging the Apache Spark configuration to use the Kryo serializer will provide performance optimizations, especially for networking-intensive applications, where large data transfers are going over the network with more complex transformations or using cloud data lake storage to persist the datasets. You can read more about the Kryo serializer in the Apache Spark Performance Tuning—Data serialization (*https://oreil.ly/kKnNJ*) documentation.

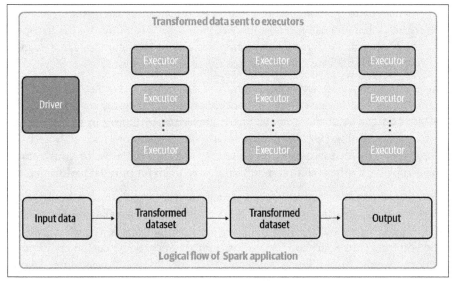

Figure 5-12. Datasets and executors in Spark application

Memory tuning

In Apache Spark, memory is used for persisting intermediate results during the transformations of data. Spark offers tuning parameters so that you can leverage how much memory is allocated to data structures. Additionally, the structure of your data can be optimized to utilize less memory. One major best practice to follow is to minimize complexities in your data structures. Keeping the data relatively flat and minimizing many nested structures can ensure that it will use less memory. As an example, you can store an address as a single string or as a structure with street address, city, state, and zip code as separate fields. Using the former means that you need less memory to understand the address. There is only one field to be read versus understanding the four fields and their relationships. A typical data structure offered by Java that is used in big data applications is a HashMap. This would utilize more memory than simpler primitive data types like arrays.

Memory management

You might wonder what the difference is between memory tuning and memory management. *Memory tuning* essentially enables you to tune how much memory is needed for your data. *Memory management* enables you to tune how you allocate available memory for different purposes. In Apache Spark, you need memory for two purposes: execution and storage. *Execution* refers to the memory needed to do computations and store the intermediate results. *Storage* refers to the caches you can leverage to store your results to minimize the network calls you need to make. Apache Spark provides a set of configurations that enables you to effectively allocate memory across the different needs.

There is probably a separate book's worth of material on Apache Spark performance tuning. This section gives you a conceptual understanding of the categories of tuning. You can read more about Spark performance tuning in the Apache Spark Performance Tuning (*https://oreil.ly/9xhOC*) documentation. I strongly recommend running PoCs with samples of datasets that are representative of your actual data usage to play with these configurations and tune them for optimal performance.

I also recommend leveraging a performance monitoring solution, either with Apache Spark monitoring (*https://oreil.ly/oWs9M*) or other tools like Datadog (*https://oreil.ly/ NCPY5*), to understand the resource utilization of your Spark job, which will in turn help you tune your Spark job for optimal performance. Some customers I know have spent more time tuning for performance than they have authoring their Spark jobs, so plan and budget for that time in your Spark job pipelines.

Minimize Overheads with Data Transfer

In a cloud data lake architecture, there are a few key things we need to remember in terms of overhead. *Overheads* are tasks or steps in your big data processing that essentially add more time to your execution, thereby deteriorating the overall performance of your cloud data lake architecture. Most of these overheads also increase the cost of your solution, so minimizing the overheads could optimize your overall costs. Following are a few key overheads:

Network calls between compute and storage

As we saw earlier, big data applications involve clusters that are constructed with VMs, as well as calls between clusters and the data lake storage, all involving network calls. These add overheads to your core job execution. Some strategies you can adopt to minimize this overhead include the following:

- Leverage caching for frequently used datasets, such as reference data or frequently read datasets, that you can store right in your cluster in memory without having to make a network call to storage.

- Write Spark applications that have an optimized query plan, leveraging partitioning, as we discussed earlier in this chapter. Reading the right amount of data required for your job, as opposed to reading more data and spending compute resources to filter that to the data you want, adds to the performance.

- Optimize for colocating your storage and compute resources. Talk to your cloud providers about the options they have for colocations.

Read or writes across region boundaries

One cardinal principle in any cloud processing is to keep the compute and storage close together. If your compute in one region needs to call into storage in another region, there is a network call made across regional boundaries. Cross-region network calls get worse in terms of performance because data has to travel a lot farther over the network. In addition, they increase the overall cost of your solution because network egress costs—costs to transfer data out of a region—are quite high compared to other costs. This is one of the patterns you need to focus on minimizing in your big data solution. If you have scenarios where you need to use datasets across regions, complete all your computations in the region where the datasets originate, and transfer only the completely processed datasets. Also evaluate if recomputing the data with local datasets is cheaper than accessing remote data or transferring data across regions.

Premium Offerings and Performance

Cloud providers often have premium offerings for their cloud services. While it is intuitive to think that paying for this premium will improve the performance and scalability of your application, it is only effective if you are using those features to solve the right problems. In this section, I want to talk about a few examples to illustrate this point with Klodars Corporation. Take the time to understand the bottlenecks and consumption patterns for your architecture, and talk to your cloud providers to determine the best fit for you. The most important consideration is to ensure that the premium offering will indeed solve your problem.

The Case of Bigger Virtual Machines

Klodars Corporation found its sales dashboards slowing down when it onboarded a new region and expanded sales. The company suspected that its compute resources were not enough and added more compute cores, vertically scaling their compute cluster. However, it observed that this did not improve the performance, and in some cases, even worsened the worst case. Upon further analysis, Klodars observed that it had partitioned its data based on time trends, and the query pattern was largely pivoting on regional trends to find the individual performance. Given that everyone was interested in the recent data, the multiple queries were all querying the recent data and later filtering for specific regions and salespersons, causing a bottleneck. Klodars changed the partition pattern to optimize for region followed by salesperson and found that this largely improved the performance.

In this case, increasing the compute cores in fact worsened the situation because there were now more queries hitting the same data. Partitioning revision was a more effective strategy.

The Case of Flash Storage

Klodars Corporation found that its product queries were getting a lot slower and saw a bottleneck in its system around slower storage transactions. It saw this offering for a storage tier based on flash storage and immediately upgraded to that. While this helped speed up the queries, Klodars immediately spotted the queries slowing again comparatively when the product data increased. This was not ideal given that the company was paying a lot more for this higher tier of storage. Upon further analysis, Klodars observed that the product data was coming from various feeds and was stored as small files. When the dataset increased, so did the number of files. This caused the metadata overhead required to read files to be much higher compared to the data. Klodars pivoted its strategy and worked on compacting these small files, which instantly increased the query performance. Klodars even went back to disk-based storage and found the performance did not regress.

In this case, the flash-drive-based storage increased the performance due to a better storage system but didn't quite solve the problem, so it returned when the dataset increased again. The right solution was to fix the antipattern around small files. Flash-based storage systems are very useful when you have a small set of data that is heavily transacted; the typical scenario here is machine learning.

Summary

In this section, I first covered the fundamentals of what performance means and how it is measured. These concepts will help you define the requirements around performance of your data lake as SLAs and SLOs as well as how you will measure these with SLIs. I then applied these concepts to cloud data lake applications and dove deep into the performance drivers of data copy and Spark applications. I also went over performance optimization strategies for these applications. Further, I talked about some of the larger patterns to consider when designing your cloud data lake solution. Finally, I discussed premium offerings and the need to understand the scenarios where the premium offerings provide benefits. With this understanding of the performance drivers of your cloud data lake architecture and the configurations and options that are available for you to tune the performance of your cloud data lake, you are ready to tweak these knobs based on which performance drivers need to be tuned in your solution.

It's important to note that this chapter provides a conceptual understanding of performance. When implementing your cloud data lake solution, I definitely recommend that you invest in the observability solution to monitor your performance and ensure that you have the right metrics and logging in place to diagnose any performance issues. This will help you put these concepts into action and measure the impact of your optimizations.

In the next chapter, I'll put this conceptual understanding of scale and performance into perspective in the context of data formats and how the data formats offer built-in optimizations for big data solutions.

CHAPTER 6

Deep Dive on Data Formats

Design is not just what it looks like and feels like. Design is how it works.

—Steve Jobs

Traditionally, data warehouses are built on a proprietary data format that they leverage to optimize for the query patterns. Given the increasing number of scenarios that are served by the cloud data lake, especially with the rise of the lakehouse architectural pattern, more and more customers and solution providers are investing in capabilities that enable running warehouse-like queries directly on the cloud data lake. This takes us close to the promise of delivering an architecture that minimizes the need to copy data back and forth across data stores for specific purposes. This promise of a data storage with no silos has resulted in an increasing number of open data formats that enable running warehouse-like queries directly on a cloud data lake storage. In this chapter, we'll take a look at three such formats: Apache Iceberg, Delta Lake, and Apache Hudi. This chapter is probably the most technical one in the book, where we look at the formats in great detail, including how they serve the scenarios they are designed for. My hope is that this chapter provides you with enough knowledge on why these formats were designed so that when you evaluate one of these formats, you can ask the right questions and find the right data format for your cloud data lake architecture.

Why Do We Need These Open Data Formats?

If I had to summarize the need for open data formats in one sentence, I would say that the open data formats essentially enable the cloud data lake storage to be able to store tabular data. This gives rise to two questions: why do we need to store tabular data, and why is it a problem to store tabular data in a cloud data lake storage? Let's explore these questions in detail.

Why Do We Need to Store Tabular Data?

In "Data Formats" on page 134, I talked about the key assumptions about data that is stored in a cloud data lake, as follows:

- Data stored in a data lake that is actively transacted is largely in a tabular format (organized as rows and columns).
- Data that is written once is read multiple times.
- The read patterns largely rely on conditional selection of data, where data that has similar values for certain columns is filtered to be returned or aggregated to be grouped.

Let's take a look at why data stored in a data lake is most commonly tabular. While data in a big data analytics system could originate from any source and be of any size and format, as illustrated by the six Vs of big data in "What Is Big Data?" on page 2, this data by itself is considered low value, riddled with a high degree of noise. The primary value proposition of a big data architecture is to generate high-value insights from this low-value data. The process of generating these high-value insights involves a variety of operations that primarily fall under a few high-level categories, listed in Table 6-1.

Table 6-1. Categories of operations on a data lake

Operation	Description	Examples from a sales dataset
Aggregation	Statistical results on a dataset	Total sales by region; maximum invoice amount closed by a salesperson
Filtering	Search for a subset of data from a large dataset that meets a specific criteria	Sales per month during summer months; customers who placed an order over a certain amount during the past year
Projection	Predict future trends based on past trends	Sales forecast for next year based on last year's trends
Joins	Correlate values from two different datasets to identify patterns	How social media trends influenced sales

A tabular data structure lends itself to these common data lake operations because it offers the flexibility to group similar data together. When similar data is grouped, it takes fewer transactions to get to the subset of the data you want and perform the computations. This is why most of the data formats optimize for storing tabular data.

In a big data analytics system, data that comes into the system need not be tabular; however, as I said before, this is considered low-value raw data. This data undergoes a set of transformations as the first step to be converted into tabular data, which is then used for further processing. You can revisit "A Day in the Life of Data" on page 73 to read more about the data lake zones. Data in zones other than the raw data zone is typically tabular in nature.

Why Is It a Problem to Store Tabular Data in a Cloud Data Lake Storage?

When you think about tabular data, it's probably intuitive for you to think of a spreadsheet that lets you organize data into rows and columns. Most databases and data warehouses have storage that is organized this way. However, as we saw in "Cloud Data Lake Storage" on page 26, the storage used by a data lake architecture is a general-purpose object storage, which is designed to store any kind of data without imposing any restrictions. So the same system used to store content that powers your websites, your blogs, and photos in your online photo album is used to store data for your big data analytics applications. The primary reasons that this is very attractive are the low cost and the ability to store data of any size and format without imposing any restrictions; this combination lets organizations bring any and all data they have to the data lake storage without breaking the bank.

At the same time, the data lake storage by itself has a few distinct limitations when it comes to storing and processing tabular data, as follows:

Updates to existing data
> Data lake storage systems are largely append-only storage systems. This means that if any of the existing data needs to be replaced, it is not a very straightforward process.

Schema enforcement and validation
> Schema refers to the description of the data itself. For example, we know that an address has the following fields—a street address, a city name, an abbreviated state, and a zip code. The object storage system does not have a way to guarantee that an address stored will have all these fields.

Query performance
> As we saw in great detail in Chapter 5, a lot of factors go into ensuring a performant data lake. However, all these factors rely on the practitioner to design for them, as opposed to an out-of-the-box guarantee, because an object storage system by itself does not guarantee performance.

Their flexibility and low cost have driven adoption of cloud data lake architectures. As a result, more business-critical queries and dashboards rely on the data residing in a general-purpose object storage. To ensure that the data stored in a general-purpose object storage system can be optimized for core data lake computations supporting the business-critical scenarios, customers and cloud data practitioners have incubated various open data formats that primarily offer guarantees on the tabular nature of the data. The compute engines that process the data also understand these open data formats, thereby ensuring an optimized performance as well. Although more and more data formats have been incubated, we will take a deeper look at three of them: Delta Lake, Apache Iceberg, and Apache Hudi.

Delta Lake

Delta Lake is an open data format incubated and maintained by Databricks, the company started by the founders of Apache Spark. As we saw in "Apache Spark" on page 31, Apache Spark enabled a unified programming model across a variety of scenarios, such as batch processing, real-time streaming, and machine learning scenarios on a unified platform in a cloud data lake architecture. The final piece of the puzzle was to remove the silo of needing a data warehouse for BI scenarios. Delta Lake was the underpinning of the data lakehouse pattern that Databricks popularized, where, in addition to batch, real-time, and machine learning scenarios, organizations could also run BI scenarios directly on the cloud data lake storage, without requiring a separate cloud data warehouse.

Why Was Delta Lake Founded?

Delta Lake was founded as the fundamental building block of the data lakehouse pattern, offering the following value propositions.

Eliminate data silos across business analysts, data scientists, and data engineers

As covered in "Apache Spark" on page 31, Apache Spark was founded on the principle of providing a flexible programming model for supporting a wide variety of applications, such as batch processing, real-time streaming, and machine learning. Apache Spark was widely successful in terms of both customer adoption and mindshare that is continuing to grow. With Apache Spark, customers could use a single programming model that worked for both data engineers for core data processing as well as data scientists for machine learning scenarios. However, there was still a need to copy data over to a data warehouse for business analysts to leverage SQL-like languages for queries because of the optimized query performance that data warehouses offered. The limitations of a cloud object storage that we discussed in "Why Do We Need These Open Data Formats?" on page 149 was the inhibitor that got in the way. Delta Lake was the open data format founded by Databricks to let business analysts leverage the cloud data lake directly for their queries, enabling a lakehouse architecture for organizations.

Provide a unified data and computational system for batch and real-time streaming data

Organizations tend to focus on two different aspects when it comes to insights: understand what is happening right now and also understand patterns from historical data. For example, when a marketing team publishes a post on social media, they would like to understand how that post is trending right now. Similarly, when they work on their next campaign, they leverage historical data to understand how the past campaigns have trended to help guide their strategy. *Real-time streaming* refers to analyzing data that enters the big data lake for immediate insights, i.e., the right now. The computations are focused on speed of processing on data that is very recent. However, if you want to have insights based on historical data, then you would work on data that is stored in the data lake with a batch processing pipeline. The architecture pattern that supports both of these paths is referred to as a *lambda architecture*, which involves a hot path for real-time analysis and a cold path for analyzing historical data. While Spark offers a unified programming language for both real-time and batch processing, analyzing real-time and historical data is traditionally done by different data pipelines. Delta Lake minimizes the need for these two different paths. A pictorial representation of the lambda architecture is shown in Figure 6-1.

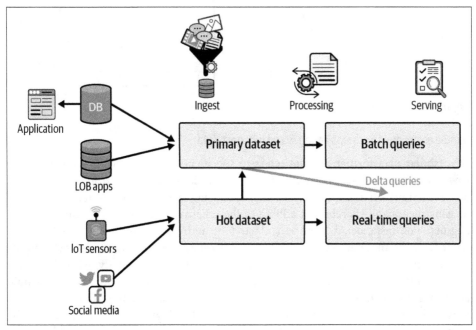

Figure 6-1. Lambda architecture

Support bulk updates or changes to existing data

As we learned earlier, data enters the data lake as low-value raw data and undergoes multiple transformations to generate high-value, structured, curated data. As the raw data changes, this affects the curated data as well. It is not uncommon for new incoming data to change multiple rows and columns in high-value curated data. As an example, let's say that there is a dataset with four rows and four columns, as shown in Figure 6-2. With new data, row A is modified, row C is deleted, and row CC is newly inserted into the table. An object data storage layer cannot handle these incremental updates to existing data in a straightforward fashion. So typically, data practitioners end up generating the whole table from scratch. As we already know, this is not ideal in terms of both cost and engineering energy spent. Further, if consumers are reading this dataset while the dataset is being recomputed, they will see inaccurate or partial results, so this recomputation needs to be orchestrated at a time that there are no readers and must be coordinated appropriately. Delta Lake offers a way to manage these incremental updates without requiring updates of the whole dataset and enables consumers of the data to continue reading the dataset while the update is being performed.

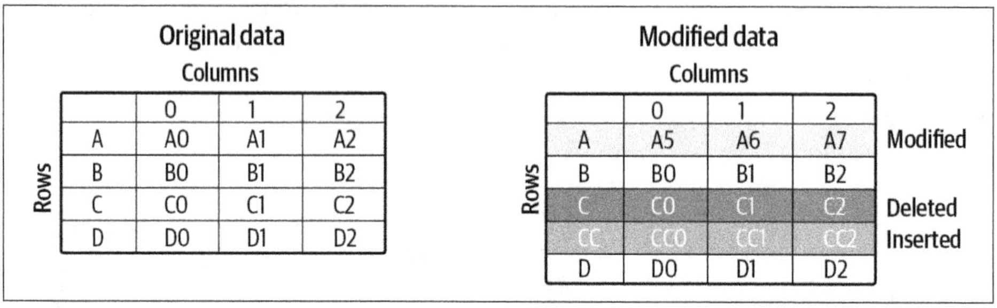

Figure 6-2. Updates to datasets

Handle errors due to schema changes and incorrect data

In a tabular data format, *schema* refers to specifications or descriptions of what the row and column values need to be. Because a cloud data lake storage system has no restrictions on the size or shape of the data, incoming data could have some missing pieces and thereby not adhere to the schema expected by the computational engines. For instance, if there is a dataset of addresses coming in, and there are records within that dataset that don't have a street address or a zip code, the compute engine extracting addresses from this dataset would fail. Similarly, with time, data sources could add new fields or change existing fields, and compute engines would get confused because there is older data and newer data in the same dataset that now look different. An example of this is provided in Figure 6-3. Delta Lake enables graceful handling of these scenarios by offering schema enforcement and schema validation, so you can ensure that checks are performed on this data and proactively rectify this by fixing the missing values with defaults or rejecting the records that don't adhere to the schema.

All this sounds amazing. How does Delta Lake enable these scenarios? Delta Lake strives to offer *ACID* guarantees of data: *a*tomicity, *c*onsistency, *i*ntegrity, and *d*urability of data in the data lake storage, laying the foundations for enabling the scenarios previously described. If you would like to know more about ACID transactions, see "Reference Architecture for the Data Lakehouse" on page 41. Let's take a look at the internals of Delta Lake and how it enables these scenarios.

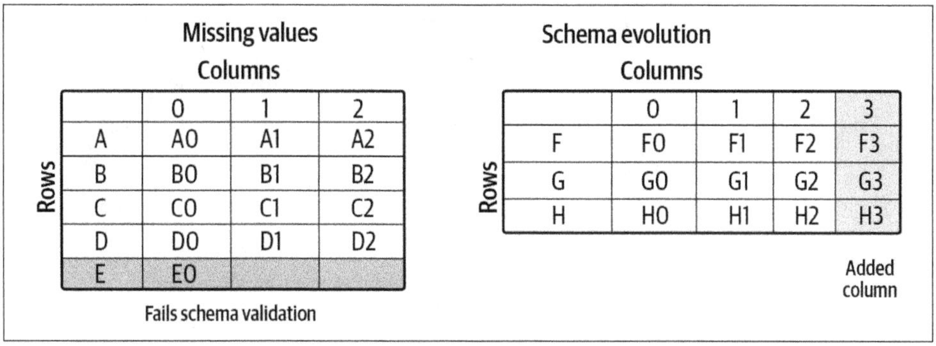

Missing values		
Columns		
	0	1	2
A	A0	A1	A2
B	B0	B1	B2
C	C0	C1	C2
D	D0	D1	D2
E	E0		

Rows

Fails schema validation

Schema evolution			
Columns			
	0	1	2	3
F	F0	F1	F2	F3
G	G0	G1	G2	G3
H	H0	H1	H2	H3

Rows

Added column

Figure 6-3. Schema validation and evolution

How Does Delta Lake Work?

Delta Lake is an open storage format used to store tabular data in data lake storage systems, offering ACID guarantees. A Delta Lake table consists of the following components:

Data objects
> The actual data in the table stored as Parquet files. You can review the concepts behind Apache Parquet in "Exploring Apache Parquet" on page 135.

Log
> A transaction log, or a ledger, that keeps track of changes to the data in the table. These changes are called *actions* and are stored in JSON format. Delta log keeps track of changes to the data itself; the inserts, deletes, or updates; and the changes to the metadata or the schema, where columns are added or removed from the table.

Log checkpoints
> A compressed version of the log that contains nonredundant actions up to a certain point in time. As you might imagine, given the number of actions that happen to data over time, the log could grow a lot, so the log checkpoints serve as an optimization for performance.

The Delta Lake documentation page (*https://oreil.ly/Zq5Nu*) provides detailed instructions for how to work with Delta tables. When you create a Delta table, a log is also created for that table. All changes to the table are recorded in the log, and this log is crucial to maintaining the integrity of the data in the table, thereby offering the guarantees we discussed.

As shown in Figure 6-4, a write to a Delta table involves two components:

- Make the updates to the data objects by modifying the Parquet files.
- Update the Delta log and associate that modification with a unique identifier in the Delta log.

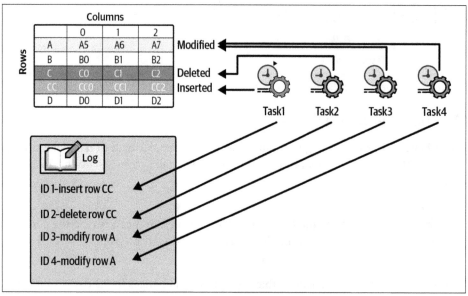

Figure 6-4. Delta lake writes

Unless both of the operations are completed, the write does not succeed. So if there are two simultaneous writes to the table, they are automatically serialized in a sequential fashion with this log. The second write needs to wait until the first write succeeds with the updates to the log, and then the second write completes by updating the log. Having this log with a transaction ledger also enables the caller to time travel, to access past versions of the data.

In addition to offering ACID guarantees and enabling scenarios like time travel, Delta tables provide schema enforcement, where you can ensure that data adheres to the schema that you specify (e.g., zip codes have to be five-digit integers), and schema evolution, where as you add new columns and evolve your schema, you can ensure the older data works by placing default values. These make SQL-like scenarios possible on the data lake.

When Do You Use Delta Lake?

Delta Lake provides stronger guarantees to data that resides in a general-purpose object storage. One thing you need to remember is that for data stored in the Delta Lake format, you need to leverage compute engines that understand the format to take advantage of its capabilities. I recommend that you leverage Delta Lake on the data that you expect to run SQL-like queries on or datasets that power machine learning models where you need to be able to preserve the versions. If you use Apache Spark, you can largely leverage your existing pipelines with minimal modifications to convert your existing data to Delta Lake format.

Apache Iceberg

Apache Iceberg was incubated by Netflix as it was powering its business-critical applications on top of the data lake storage, with the shortcomings described in "Why Is It a Problem to Store Tabular Data in a Cloud Data Lake Storage?" on page 151.

Why Was Apache Iceberg Founded?

Netflix is a popular video-streaming company that was built as a highly data-driven company since its inception. Data powers its critical business scenarios, such as providing recommendations to users based on their watching patterns, understanding the kind of content Netflix needs to create or distribute to engage its user base, and monitoring the health of its services, to name a few. Especially in a highly competitive space like video streaming with multiple players in the market, data-driven insights and business are one of Netflix's key differentiators.

According to the Netflix technology blog (*https://oreil.ly/QX_dh*), the datasets used in Netflix reside in different data stores: Amazon S3, which is a general-purpose object storage powering its cloud data lake; MySQL, which is an operational database; and Redshift and Snowflake, which are data warehouses, to name a few. The data platform at Netflix ensures that these diverse data stores are interoperable as one single data warehouse to its consumers. This is depicted in Figure 6-5.

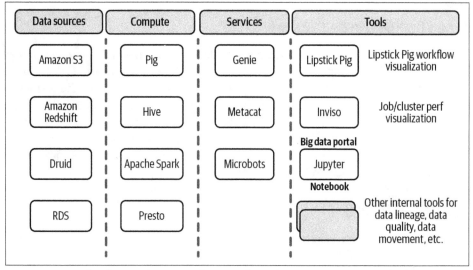

Figure 6-5. Netflix data architecture diagram from their technology blog (https://oreil.ly/QX_dh)

Specifically on the data that resides in its cloud data lake on Amazon S3, Netflix leverages Apache Hive tables (*https://oreil.ly/fS5yN*), which enabled a table format using the Apache Hadoop ecosystem to run SQL-like queries. Netflix ran into the following limitations with the general-purpose object storage solution:

Updates to existing datasets
As we saw earlier in "Why Was Delta Lake Founded?" on page 152, object storage systems do not handle changes to existing data well. Strong consistency refers to the behavior where a read-always returns the data that was last written. AWS announced strongly consistent writes in 2020 (*https://oreil.ly/-n8Bf*). However, at the time Apache Iceberg was founded, Amazon S3 offered eventually consistent writes, which did not provide predictable data on reads to Netflix users. To overcome this, the writes needed to be coordinated and orchestrated in a fashion that did not conflict with the reads.

Performance of Apache Hive
Apache Hive stored the data in files and folders on the object storage file system. This meant that any time data needed to be queried, the files and folders needed to be listed to find the data of interest. As the size of the data grew to a petabyte scale, the need to list files at that scale became really expensive and created performance bottlenecks for the queries.

Apache Iceberg was incubated as an open source project in 2018 to overcome these restrictions of using tables on a cloud data lake.

How Does Apache Iceberg Work?

Apache Iceberg, interestingly, builds on top of existing data formats, so you could use it on top of your existing data. The physical data is stored in open data formats like Apache Parquet and Apache ORC. The simplest way to describe Apache Iceberg is that it is a translation layer between the physical storage of data (Apache Parquet or Apache ORC) and how it comes together and is structured to form a logical table.

Apache Iceberg stores the files that contribute to the table in a persistent tree structure. The state of the table is stored in multiple files that describe the metadata, as follows:

- A catalog file that has the pointers to the latest version of the metadata and is the primary source of truth for where the latest version of the metadata is
- A snapshot metadata file that stores the metadata about the table, such as the schema, the partitioning structure, and so on
- A manifest list for this snapshot, where there is an entry for each manifest file associated with the snapshot
- A set of manifest files that contains a list of paths to the files that actually store the data as well as metrics about the data itself, such as the minimum and maximum values of columns in the dataset

This manifest also contains the metadata about the datasets, such as the upper and lower bounds of columns, similar to the row group headers. This is depicted in Figure 6-6.

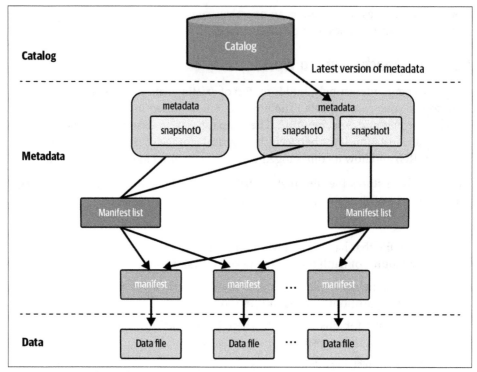

Figure 6-6. Apache Iceberg structure

Let's go over an example of how Apache Iceberg does writes, as illustrated in Figure 6-7.

As you can see, initially the Apache Iceberg table has rows A, B, C, and D and is stored across two data files. There are manifest files that point to these data files and a manifest list that contains pointers to these two manifest files. Let me walk you through the sequence of how a change to this dataset is managed in Apache Iceberg:

- When row A is modified first, that data is written in a new data file, and a new manifest file is created to point to this new row. A new snapshot is created and preserved in a manifest list file. Apache Iceberg then updates the catalog to point to this new manifest list file. The write succeeds when all of these succeed, and the writes are completed only when the catalog file updates the metadata pointer to the newest version; this controls multiple writes.

- When row C is deleted and row CC is inserted, a similar process is repeated, and the catalog now points to the newest version of the data.

- When there is a read query that filters only for rows A and B, the manifest files help indicate that the data files containing rows CC and D can be skipped, thereby avoiding unnecessary reads of files and increasing query performance.

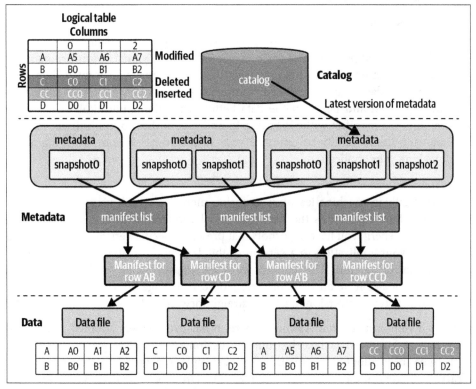

Figure 6-7. Writes using Apache Iceberg

The Apache Iceberg wiki (*https://oreil.ly/FLHAy*) has detailed documentation on how to use Apache Iceberg.

When Do You Use Apache Iceberg?

Similar to Delta Lake, Apache Iceberg is used for curated data and enriched data zones, where data assumes a tabular format, and also for queries. Prioritize the data where strong guarantees are expected. Since this is update heavy, typically this is the curated data zone in the table. Apache Iceberg is best suited for when you need structural guarantees on your data without having to require a specific format to be used for your underlying data. Apache Iceberg offers the following capabilities that you can leverage in your architecture:

Support for schema evolution

When the schema is updated—that is, new columns are added or existing columns are deleted—these updates are preserved in the snapshots, and you can leverage them to understand how the schema has evolved over time.

Data partition optimization

As we saw in "Data Formats" on page 134, placing similar data closer together offers increased performance for your queries because you are optimizing for the smallest number of transactions to get to the data that you want. When your underlying data changes, you can continue making changes to how the data files are organized and partition the data better, while the applications continue to call into the manifest without having to understand these optimizations, thereby allowing the flexibility to optimize your data layouts without worrying about breaking your applications.

Time travel or rollback

Specifically in machine learning scenarios, models are built using a certain version of the data, and as the data changes, the model behavior also changes. In Apache Iceberg, you have snapshots that preserve specific versions of data, so you can tie your application to a version of the data by associating it with a specific snapshot or version. This concept is called *snapshot isolation*. Further, if your newer updates have an issue or error, you can manage your snapshots and roll back to a previous version in a more straightforward fashion.

Although Netflix incubated Apache Iceberg, it has been widely adopted as an open data format for the data lake by multiple customers and data providers. Apache Iceberg has been adopted by organizations like Apple, Airbnb, LinkedIn, and Expedia Travel. In addition, data platform providers like Dremio, Snowflake, and AWS have provided native support for Apache Iceberg in their cloud offerings.

Apache Iceberg is very similar to Delta Lake in offering a tabular structure for your data in the data lake; however, the way it accomplishes that is with the metadata layer. Apache Iceberg supports non-Parquet file formats as well, so if you need data in varied formats to have a tabular representation, Apache Iceberg works great. With features like scan planning (*https://oreil.ly/Et3KI*), you can greatly optimize the performance of operating on large datasets by quickly narrowing the dataset(s) of interest for the query.

Apache Hudi

Apache Hudi was incubated by Uber, a company that started as one of the first ride-sharing applications. Over the years, Uber has evolved into a mobility-as-a-service provider, offering additional services like food delivery (Uber Eats and Postmates), package delivery, couriers, freight transportation, electric bicycle and motorized scooter rental via a partnership with Lime, and ferry transport in partnership with local operators. The underpinning of this rapid expansion of Uber lies in the data-driven culture that is part of the DNA of the organization. Data and advanced machine learning capabilities power critical Uber business operations, such as predicting drivers' estimated times of arrival, making meaningful recommendations to Uber customers for ordering their next dinner, and ensuring rider and passenger safety, to name a few. The timeliness of these features—that is, the real-time recommendations or actions—are critical to ensuring a great customer experience. This, of course, is important for Uber's customer satisfaction and branding. Faced by challenges that were similar to those faced by Netflix, in addition to other challenges involving the importance of real-time insights, Uber incubated Apache Hudi to offer strong guarantees and timely insights on data that resides in a data lake. Apache Hudi was designed to support these operations and data guarantees at scale, supporting around 500 billion record updates per data on a 150 PB data lake as of the year 2020, which is only growing as Uber continues to scale as a business.

Why Was Apache Hudi Founded?

The motivations for Apache Hudi are largely similar to those for Apache Iceberg and Delta Lake, in that it was founded to overcome the inherent limitations of the general-purpose object storage used to power the data lake storage. Specifically, Uber wanted to address the following scenarios:

Upserts for efficient writes
> *Upsert* refers to a concept where data needs to be written as an insert operation when it doesn't already exist or as an update operation if the row already exists. In a scenario where upserts are not supported, there are multiple rows instead of one, and a separate computation needs to be written to fetch these rows and filter for the most recent data. This solution costs more as well as takes more time for processing. Object storage systems are largely append only, and they do not inherently support the concept of upserts.

Understand incremental modifications
> As we saw in previous chapters, data processing pipelines run jobs that process large numbers of datasets to generate highly curated data that constitutes aggregated, filtered, and joined versions of the input data. Typically, whenever the input data is changed, these processing engines recompute the curated data over the entire dataset. To speed up the time to insights, instead of reprocessing the whole batch, there was an opportunity to run the recomputations only on the datasets that changed, thereby processing only the incremental changes. To do this, there was a need to understand what had changed since the last job, and this operation is not naturally supported by the data lake storage as is.

Support real-time insights

As we saw in "Why Was Delta Lake Founded?" on page 152, while there are programming models that offer unified computation across real-time and batch streaming, the actual architectures and implementations are different. As an example, when there are decisions to be made, such as finding the best drivers to call for a particular ride, the real-time data about the driver location is combined with the batch data of maps and traffic optimizations to book the best driver. Similarly, when serving recommendations in Uber Eats, the real-time clickstream data of what the customer is browsing at that moment is combined with the recommendations data, which is possibly in a graph database, to serve the right recommendations. Once again, the data lake storage as is was not natively designed for these scenarios.

Apache Hudi was primarily designed to drive efficiencies with support for upserts and incremental processing that enable data freshness in minutes as opposed to recomputing the entire dataset from scratch.

How Does Apache Hudi Work?

Apache Hudi, like other formats, is an open data format that is used to store tabular data. In a lambda architecture that supports both real-time streaming scenarios and batch scenarios, you have two kinds of write patterns on the data:

- Continuous ingestion of large volumes of data—think of a ton of Uber vehicles transmitting information in real time.
- Batch ingestion of data in bulk—think of dumps of sales or marketing data that are done with daily jobs.

To support these patterns, Apache Hudi offers two kinds of tables:

Copy on write

There is one source of truth that both readers and writers of the table interact with. Every write is immediately written as an update to the Apache Hudi table, and the updates are reflected in near real time to the readers. The data is stored in a columnar format optimized for reads, such as Apache Parquet.

Merge on read

Every write is written into a buffered zone in a write-optimized data format (a row-based data format such as Apache Avro), and this is later updated to the table that serves the readers, where data is stored in a columnar format (such as Apache Parquet).

Apache Hudi consists of three main components that are stored for a table:

Data files
The files containing the actual data. For copy-on-write tables, the data is stored in a columnar format. For merge-on-read tables, data is stored as a combination of incremental writes stored in row-based formats and the full dataset stored in columnar formats.

Metadata files
This is a complete set of all transactions stored as an ordered timeline of activities on a table. There are four types of transactions on an Apache Hudi table:

Commits
An atomic write operation of a batch of records into a dataset stored in an Apache Hudi table.

Delta commits
An atomic write operation of a batch of records into a delta log, which needs to later be committed to the dataset; this operation is supported only on the merge-on-read type of tables.

Compaction
A background process of optimizing data stored by reorganizing its file structure, where the delta files are merged into the columnar format in the dataset.

Cleans
A background process where older versions of data that are no longer required are deleted.

Index
A data structure that enables efficient lookups of the data files belonging to the transactions.

Three types of reads are supported on Apache Hudi tables:

Snapshot queries
Query a specific snapshot of the data stored in the Apache Hudi table. A *snapshot* refers to the version of the data for a given time. This query returns all the data that matches your query.

Delta queries
Query data that has changed over a given time period. If you are only interested in what changed, you will use delta queries.

Read optimized queries

This query type is supported for the merge-on-read tables and returns the data that is stored in a format optimized for reads. This does not include the data in the delta files that is not yet compacted. This query is optimized for faster performance and comes with the trade-off of data not being the freshest.

Let's put these concepts together and walk through a concrete example of how Apache Hudi works.

Copy-on-write tables

A pictorial representation of the transactions on the copy-on-write tables is given in Figure 6-8.

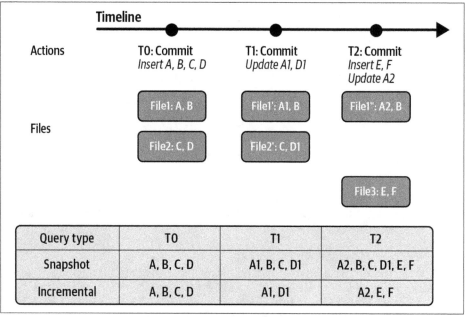

Figure 6-8. Transactions on copy-on-write tables

In the copy-on-write tables, every write—whether it is an insert operation where new rows are inserted, an update operation where existing rows are updated, or a delete operation where existing rows are deleted—is treated as a commit. There is one source of truth for the dataset preserved in a columnar format, and every write is an atomic operation where the dataset is updated. Snapshots of this truth are preserved, where you see what the data was at a particular point in time. The queries supported here are snapshot and delta queries.

Merge-on-read tables

A pictorial representation of the transactions on the merge-on-read tables is shown in Figure 6-9. Although this is mostly similar to copy-on-write tables, as shown in Figure 6-8, the key difference here is that the source of truth is distributed.

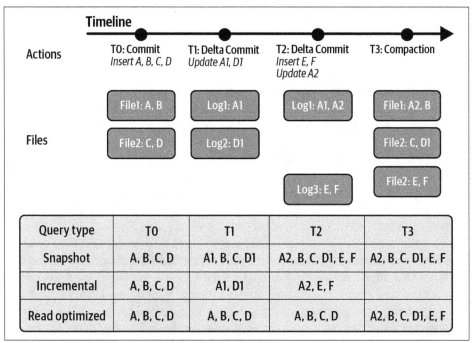

Figure 6-9. Transactions on merge-on-read tables

In the merge-on-read tables, there is a dataset in a columnar data format optimized for reads, and writes are stored in delta logs in a write-optimized format, which are then compacted into the primary dataset in a columnar format. Three types of queries are supported on these tables: a snapshot query that returns the version of the dataset as of a particular time, a delta query that returns only the data that changed, and a read-optimized query that returns the dataset from the columnar format, which offers faster performance but does not include the data that has not yet been compacted.

When Do You Use Apache Hudi?

Apache Hudi offers more flexibility with its different types of tables that support different types of queries while providing strong data guarantees with atomic writes and versioning of data. Apache Hudi was incubated by Uber but since then has been gaining strong adoption across other companies, such as Amazon, Walmart,

Disney+ Hotstar, GE Aviation, Robinhood, and TikTok. A recently founded company, Onehouse (*https://oreil.ly/DeGXF*), offers a managed platform built on Apache Hudi.

Apache Hudi is designed to support tables that need to handle a high frequency of writes in both real-time and batch fashion. It also offers the flexibility of using different types of queries based on the requirements you have for performance and data freshness.

Summary

In this chapter, we dove deeper into the data formats and built an understanding of how these data formats offer strong guarantees of data while helping improve query performance, and keep the cost profile low by leveraging the data lake storage. I went over what Delta Lake is and how it can be used. I also described data formats that were incubated by customers running large-scale data lakes: Apache Iceberg and Apache Hudi. These open data formats enable a truly no-silo data lake, which can support a variety of computations, meeting the needs of data engineers, machine learning engineers, data scientists, and BI analysts on one platform. In spite of the leaps made with these data formats, steep learning skills and a strong data platform team are required to build your data lake leveraging these data formats. Data solution providers like Dremio, AWS, and Onehouse are building managed data platform solutions that offer lakehouse out of the box. Tabular is a relatively new organization that offers a data platform based on Apache Iceberg. Depending on the motivations and engineering resources of your organization, you can make lakehouse a reality on a cloud data lake. In the next chapter, we'll focus on the end-to-end decision-making strategies by putting together all the concepts we have covered in these first six chapters.

CHAPTER 7

Decision Framework for Your Architecture

Truly successful decision-making relies on a balance between deliberate and instinctive thinking.

—Malcolm Gladwell

With the content in the prior chapters, I've covered the fundamental concepts of designing the architecture of big data processing on the cloud, the different architecture choices for big data lakes, design considerations for your cloud data lake solution, and the tools you have available to optimize your solution for scale and performance. In this chapter, I will put all of these concepts together and elaborate on how this understanding serves you at different points on your data lake journey. In building as well as consuming these cloud data lake solutions, I have talked to hundreds of customers across various industries—financial services, retail, consumer goods, health care, manufacturing, and technology sectors. This chapter distills the experiences of all these customers into a core set of common patterns and thought processes reflecting different levels of organizational maturity, available skill sets, and current states of technology adoption.

Although each of these customers has its own arc of problems and requirements, the common thread for every one of them is that they realize the importance of data and how it can help inform and transform their businesses. Data is viewed as a fundamental component to maintain their competitive advantage, retain and grow their customer base, and drive efficiencies in their operations. In this chapter, we'll take a deeper look at how the concepts are applied in the context of the consumer's problems.

I will provide a decision framework that is broken down into four key phases: assess, define, implement, and operationalize. In Chapter 3, I talked about this decision framework at a higher level, and in this chapter, I'll tune this framework to the segments that you belong to. These steps are sequential; however, you can always go back to the previous phase as you discover gaps when you are in a later phase. I have also provided a set of templates that you can use to plan and track the different phases of your cloud data lake in the Appendix.

Cloud Data Lake Assessment

The very first step in any project is to understand and orient yourself with respect to where you are and where you want to go. To tackle this, I'll kick off this conversation with a set of questions that will help you orient yourself on where you currently are and what your motivations are for the cloud data lake.

When taking this assessment, you are playing the role of the data platform team or the data architect for your organization. Regardless of what your actual role is—CTO, engineering manager, architect, or senior engineer—represent this role as best you can as it applies to your organization. I have structured this assessment in a multiple-choice format. For every question, pick the option that most closely aligns with your situation and needs. There are legitimate circumstances where more than one option fits your needs. What I recommend in that case is to segment your problem space into subproblems and perform an assessment for each subproblem to identify the best fit. If you don't know the answer to a question, I recommend doing enough investigations to get a rough idea—remember, progress is better than perfection.

Once you have taken this assessment, as you go through the other sections of the book based on the option that describes you best, focus on the aspects of those areas that I have called out that specifically represent that option.

Cloud Data Lake Assessment Questionnaire

All right, it's time now. Ready, set, go!

Q1: Does your organization currently have an investment in data analytics?

Option A
> We don't have a huge investment in data today and are almost starting from a blank slate. Maybe if I squint hard enough, I can say that our current data investments are in the form of a few databases that power our applications.

Option B
> Yes, we have an on-premises data warehouse such as the equivalent of Netezza or Oracle RAC servers or on-premises Hadoop clusters.

Option C
> We have a cloud data lake or cloud data warehouse, or both, today that is functional and serving our organization.

Q2: How would you best describe the skill levels of your data organization?

Option A

We have some existing folks taking on the responsibilities of data as a part-time effort. Our focus is to keep the lights on, and we handle the investments reactively as someone raises a request.

Option B

We have an existing data organization, which is currently occupied with operationally managing our data infrastructure and data pipelines. We run the organization's data needs. Typical titles in our data platform organization are data administrator, data engineer, and data analyst.

Option C

We have a highly technical data organization that stays current on the latest cloud offerings. We believe in automating operational tasks and actively work on removing bottlenecks while scaling to our organization's data needs.

Q3: How would you best describe the load levels of your data organization?

Option A

The data organization is largely focused on keeping the lights on, with no strong dependencies.

Option B

The data organization is critical to serving the needs of the entire organization and is constantly overloaded with requests from all over as well as with the work required to keep the data platform up and running.

Option C

The data organization is critical to my organization for core tasks around managing and operating the data lake. However, they make the data available so they don't bottleneck their customers on their capacity.

Q4: What is the rough size of the data in your data platform?

Option A

None at all, maybe a few terabytes of data

Option B

A few hundred terabytes to a petabyte

Option C

Multiple petabytes

Q5: How would you best describe your customers?

Option A

My customers rely on us to educate them about how data can help them. Otherwise, this is not quite top of their mind.

Option B

My customers are mostly business analysts and executives who consume our reports and dashboards. They depend on the data for their operations.

Option C

My customers are engineers, data scientists, business analysts, and executives who rely on data to be available to them for their growing needs.

Q6: How you would best describe the data awareness and skill sets of your customers?

Option A

My customers don't necessarily think about the data. Data needs, if any, for our customers are more means to the end to completing their tasks, such as databases powering their applications.

Option B

My customers rely on data heavily but are not skilled at coding or data technologies. They rely on the data team to prepare dashboards and reports end to end.

Option C

My customers are highly technical and cloud savvy. They may consume some dashboards and reports generated by the data team, but they go beyond that in doing their own analysis.

Analysis for Your Cloud Data Lake Assessment

At a very high level, depending on where the majority of your answers are, you fall under one of the three buckets shown in Figure 7-1:

- If you mostly picked **Option A**, then you are almost new to the data lake and are starting from a blank slate.
- If you mostly picked **Option B**, you have an existing data lake or a data warehouse. Your cloud data lake implementation involves addressing existing technical debts as well as making a cultural shift in your organization's data culture.
- If you mostly picked **Option C**, then you already have a cloud data lake implementation, and your efforts are to make an existing implementation better, faster, and more efficient.

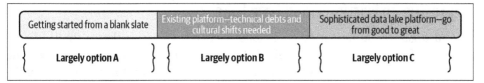

Getting started from a blank slate	Existing platform—technical debts and cultural shifts needed	Sophisticated data lake platform—go from good to great
Largely option A	Largely option B	Largely option C

Figure 7-1. Data platform assessment for your organization

Let's take a look at what these mean in greater detail.

Starting from Scratch

If you are new to data lakes or the cloud or both of them—that is, if you are starting your journey from scratch—you will first focus on bounding your highly open problem space to what really matters to your organization. This will define the subsequent requirements for design, implementation, and operationalization of your cloud data lake. In addition to scoping this problem space, you likely will also have to pitch to your business leaders how an investment in the data lake will move the needle on your business. The good news is you have little to no technical debt to pay off, and the efforts are more aligned with value and impact as they apply to the needs of your organization. If your organization does not have an existing data platform team, which is possibly because this is your first foray into data lakes, you may have to leverage existing software engineering or IT organizations to play the role of the data platform team. Based on these learnings, you can plan to bootstrap the data team within your organization.

Migrating an Existing Data Lake or Data Warehouse to the Cloud

If your organization has an existing data warehouse or a data lake running on-premises that is already serving the organization's data needs, this will be a great starting point for the team to realize the helpfulness of data, and the wins here already help your business leaders understand the value of data. You also likely have an existing data platform team; however, it is highly probable that this team is mostly focused on operations and has a high degree of load. In addition to focusing the core data-focused initiatives, your data platform team is working on maintaining the data centers and the software running on premises. Your efforts on the cloud data lake will need to factor in the existing solutions you support with your current data lake or data warehouse as well as drive new opportunities and solve other problems with data. One of the important factors in your decision is ensuring that you minimize disruptions for your customers as you migrate your data platform to the cloud. Your efforts around migration also involve upskilling your data platform team to design and operationalize for the cloud.

Improving an Existing Cloud Data Lake

If your organization has an existing cloud data lake, your situation is similar to the segment of customers running their data lake or data warehouse on premises, the primary difference being that you already have a presence on the cloud. Your problems are focused on either improving your cloud data lake architecture to address existing scenarios on your data lake or adding completely new scenarios that provide differentiated value to your customers. The cloud data lake is a rapidly evolving field, so your decisions need to be grounded in the problems you face in your current implementation as well as the opportunities that new innovations on the cloud data lake could bring to your organization. As in the previous scenario, it is important that your efforts cause minimal disruption to your existing customers. From an organizational perspective, your data platform team is already familiar with the cloud, and upskilling primarily is to keep up with the innovations happening in the data lake area.

Importance of the Assess Phase

An important aspect to remember here is that investing in the assess phase is critical to derisking your data lake design, implementation, and release. Take your time to build the prioritization and stakeholder alignment with your customers and business leaders. Although you may not know everything and things will change, an initial list of prioritized requirements and stakeholder buy-in ensure that changes are managed appropriately.

In the upcoming sections, I will walk through the decision process of each of these scenarios with our fictitious Klodars Corporation. Please note that Klodars Corporation will assume multiple personalities in terms of data organization and maturity to best illustrate the current state and requirements of the representative customer segment. I will go through the phases of the decision framework as they apply to the three different segments: getting started from scratch, migrating an existing data lake or warehouse to the cloud, and improving on an existing cloud data lake. Figure 7-2 provides a quick overview of this framework.

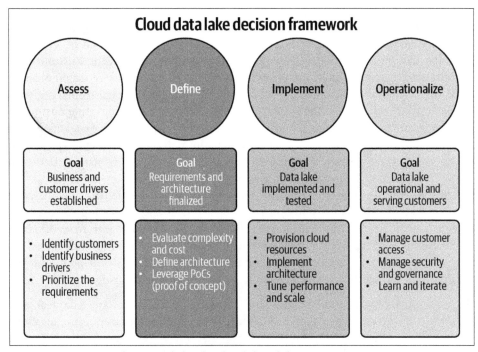

Figure 7-2. Decision framework for the cloud data lake

Setting for Klodars Corporation

Klodars Corporation is an organization selling rain gear and umbrellas to other retail outlets as well as directly to customers through its website. Its website is powered by an operational data-store. Klodars is motivated to invest in a cloud data lake architecture to better support the expansion and growth of its business. The data platform team will define, build, launch, and operate the cloud data lake to serve the needs of the company. The customers of this data platform are various divisions within Klodars that leverage data to drive product or business insights.

Phase 1 of Decision Framework: Assess

The objective of this phase is to define and prioritize the requirements for the cloud data lake that will drive the architecture and implementation decisions. In this phase, the data engineering team needs to identify the requirements based on two key aspects: customer requirements and business drivers.

Understand Customer Requirements

Identify who your customers are and their current pain points that can be addressed with the data lake. A great way to kick this off is by interviewing customers to understand what their goals are and what barriers get in the way of accomplishing their goals. Now, how do you know who your customers are? The customers of your data lake are anyone who could benefit from data. They could be the either customers of your organization who use your products or other departments or teams within your organization. They could benefit from data in multiple ways: they may use it to make their current operations more efficient, identify patterns or insights that help them focus on new strategies, and/or generate new monetization opportunities by offering insights to their customer, to name a few. For example, the customers of the data lake in Klodars Corporation could be the sales and marketing departments within Klodars or the wholesale distributors that buy the rain gear from Klodars. Some examples of the benefits include the ability for the retailers to understand the demand for the products to manage their inventories efficiently or the ability for the internal teams to figure out new sales strategies or marketing campaigns.

An important thing to remember is that not all your customers are technical, and they may not necessarily realize how a data lake helps them. Keep your questions open-ended, and focus on their problems or barriers to better understand where data can help them. The following list provides a set of questions that can help identify these constraints or problems:

- What are your business objectives? What is getting in the way of accomplishing them?
- Who are your customers? How do you anticipate their needs?
- Tell me more about your customer adoption, engagement, and retention. How do you manage these, and how do you understand the effect of your investments on the customer journey?
- When something goes wrong with your sales or revenue, how do you understand what happened, and how do you fix that?
- How do you differentiate yourself from your competitors? How do you understand these strategies?
- What are the current inefficiencies in your operations? How are you addressing them today? What could be done better?
- What are the bottlenecks in your processes today? What is in your critical path, and how does it affect your business and operations?

These questions are a good starting point, and you can choose to customize them or derive insights based on your specific problems. The primary signals you want to capture are areas where your customers do not have enough visibility into the problems, or the root causes or areas that require a lot of laborious effort to get visibility or understanding.

Understand Opportunities for Improvement

This primarily applies to customers who have a current data platform or data warehouse on the cloud or running on premises. If you are building your cloud data lake from scratch, you can skip this section and go to "Know Your Business Drivers" on page 178.

As mentioned in the previous section, the first step is to start with understanding your data lake customers as well as your data platform team's current pain points. The objective of this section is to understand and prioritize the problems of running your existing data platform that could be addressed with the cloud data lake.

As an example, Klodars Corporation's sales team uses dashboards built by the data platform team for daily executive reviews as well as to determine sales projections and targets. However, there are multiple instances during peak-season or high-load times when the executive reviews are disrupted because the dashboards were not refreshed on time, and this problem ends up hurting the sales team's credibility as well as increasing the data platform team's load in addressing these escalations and customer issues. Similarly, the marketing team needs to run targeted campaigns on social media and wants to analyze the trends, which the current set of tools, platforms, and data analysts doesn't support. The team would like to have data scientists help identify patterns and trends over social media feeds.

The following list provides a set of questions that can help identify these problems:

To your customers

- How is data helping you accomplish your business objectives? What could be done better?
- If there were no restrictions based on feasibility, what kinds of data and insights would you like to leverage in your decision making?
- Are there requirements for the data platform that have not been met? What are the obstacles? How does that affect your business objectives? What are you doing about it?
- Are you getting your insights from data in a timely fashion? What would be the impact if we were to provide these insights faster?
- How much of your effort is needed to realize value from your data? Are there opportunities to lower this even further? If we did, how would that help you with your business objectives?

To your data platform team

- How much effort and time are spent on your data operations today? How does that affect your load and morale? What could be done better?

- What is the cost of running your data operations today? If you were to lower this cost, how would that help your operations?

- What kind of data do you work with today? Do you find that this limiting your potential? What other data do you want to bring into your organization, and how would that help your business and customers?

At the end of this exercise, you'll have a very clear idea of the needs of your customers as well as the effort and investments required to support these scenarios.

Know Your Business Drivers

Your customer interviews tell you about the problems that data can help with. The business drivers help prioritize these problems. The business drivers are a set of conditions, resources, or processes that are critical to the continued growth and success of the business. Some common business drivers include the following:

Reduce the cost of running the business
   This includes the cost of people, resources, and tools involved in building the products as well as operating the business. For instance, in the case of Klodars Corporation, this is the cost of manufacturing the rain gear, operating and maintaining the warehouses and distribution channels for the rain gear, and paying the employees to operate the company across the departments.

Reduce risk
   This includes risks introduced to your data lake due to issues such as poor security implementation, data quality, or data governance, which end up increasing the cost of operations as well as affecting the top-line business metrics of your organization. For instance, in the case of Klodars Corporation, lack of data quality checks in the sales data results in trends in the executive dashboards that give the perception that profits have taken a nosedive, when in fact it is a data error.

Increase the efficiency of operations
   This effort primarily targets reducing the time and resources it takes to produce a business outcome with existing tools and processes. As an example, Klodars Corporation needs to maintain an inventory of rain gear to ensure that it has the products ready when customers want them. At the same time, if there is too much inventory compared to the demand, then goods are sitting idle in its warehouses, eating into its profit margins. An effort focused on efficiency here would be to accurately predict the demand, called *demand forecasting*, to ensure

that you strike the sweet spot where customers have the products when they want them, and you don't have too many goods in your inventory.

Drive innovations to differentiate your business and products
This effort can be best described as seeing round the corner—that is, taking steps to address the unknown while derisking this approach as much as you can. Some efforts in this category involve building a new business or product line. As an example, Klodars Corporation is currently selling rain gear in the Pacific Northwest area and has saturated the market. Klodars could drive innovations by understanding tourists in the area and investing in a rain gear rental business, expanding beyond the Pacific Northwest region, or adding new product lines around winter gear.

Complete the Assess Phase by Prioritizing the Requirements

Once you understand your customer problems, you can evaluate these problems under two dimensions:

Helpfulness of data
How can you help minimize or completely solve these problems with data, and how feasible is this solution?

Severity of the problem
How severe is this problem as compared to the business drivers of your organization? Remember that severity isn't always bad or indicates that something is broken; it can also be good by helping to add differentiated value to your business.

As we saw briefly in "Identify Your Goals" on page 64, you can now plot these problems across the two dimensions to understand what gives you the best return on investment. As a recap, I'm refreshing your memory with Figure 7-3. You can also bring your customers along as stakeholders to help work with them to address their solutions. At the end of the assess phase, you will have a prioritized list of requirements ready for your cloud data lake.

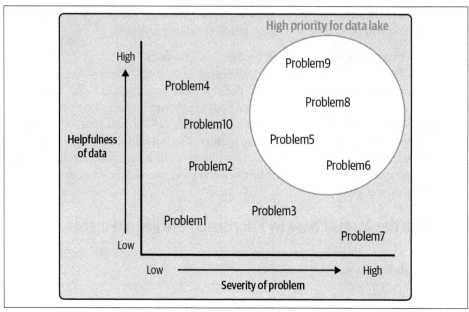

Figure 7-3. Assess problems based on severity to business and helpfulness of data

The prioritized list of requirements provides an excellent starting point for you to plan the data lake. Expect changes to this as you move ahead with your design and implementation. You may experience new headwinds that affect your prioritization or discover new customer needs that you may have missed before. A good rule of thumb is to aim for 60%–70% accuracy and completeness and target a one- to two-year time horizon, so you have a solid-enough plan that is also adaptable to any new changes.

Phase 2 of Decision Framework: Define

At the end of Phase 1, you will have a prioritized list of requirements that you will use to define and implement your cloud data lake. In Phase 2, you will define and plan the technical components that are used to build the cloud data lake. The key objectives of this phase are to complete the technical design and project plan that are required to meet the customer and business requirements determined in the assess phase. This plan then helps scope the time and resource requirements for the project.

As a quick recap of the design considerations we discussed in "Plan Your Architecture and Deliverables" on page 67, the following factors serve as a guide to determining the right architecture for your cloud data lake:

Total cost of the solution
    A data lake is very inexpensive in terms of operations but costs more in terms of development effort to build your solution. The development cost is high here

because you will be assembling your solution with different compute and storage components, as opposed to getting a ready-to-use solution. In addition, the data lake supports more scenarios than a data warehouse. As an example, in the case of Klodars Corporation, the marketing team wants to predict trends in social media. Investing in a cloud data lake would support ad hoc exploratory analytics with machine learning and data science.

Time taken to do the implementation

You may have business constraints that determine the timelines of your projects. As an example, Klodars Corporation has on-premises hardware supporting its operational datastores, which is reaching its end of life. Moving to the cloud ensures that the team can save costs in procuring new hardware; however, the time left on the existing hardware becomes a forcing function to get the cloud data lake live. If you don't have much time, reusing existing development efforts on the cloud would ensure that you get your cloud data lake faster, in comparison to rearchitecture. Another factor that could determine your timelines is to line up your data lake timelines with time-sensitive customer commitments. As an example, the sales team at Klodars Corporation needs to deliver its quarterly inventory and sales report to its top retailers in time for budgeting the projections for the next fiscal year. Enabling this as a dashboard is one of the critical requirements that the data lake needs to meet as a deliverable.

Backward compatibility

If you have an existing data lake or data warehouse solution, an important factor to consider is ensuring minimal disruption to your existing customers. The architecture patterns and deliverables need to factor in this backward compatibility until the customers can move over. As an example, applications that power the website at Klodars Corporation rely on the operational database running on premises. When Klodars Corporation moves to the cloud data lake, there is a need to support these applications until they can also migrate to the cloud. One way of achieving this is to keep the operational database on premises and take daily backups to the cloud data lake as part of the data ingestion.

Organizational maturity

Cloud data lakes, as we saw, require relatively high skill sets; factor that in when making architecture choices. You can factor in time to hire or upskill (or both) development teams to implement the cloud data lake. Additionally, you can hire system integrators who can help you with implementing a cloud data lake. Most cloud providers have close collaborations with system integrators and can provide you with a list of recommendations. As an example, to accomplish the marketing team's goal of implementing analysis of social media data, you need to have data scientists in place who can do this analysis in addition to the technology choices.

With this in mind, there are two outcomes in Phase 2:

- Technical design choices are finalized for the cloud data lake.
- A project plan is in place with scope, dependencies, and timelines that can be communicated to your stakeholders.

> **Timelines for Your Cloud Data Lake**
>
> I hear from my customers often about how long it will take to implement the cloud data lake once the architecture is finalized. This timeline largely depends on three factors: the complexity of your architecture, the implementation choices for the cloud services you are choosing, and the skill levels of your team. A good rule of thumb is, as you define your project deliverables, identify rough timelines for the efforts as T-shirt size estimates, as follows:
>
> - XS is less than one week
> - S is one to two weeks
> - M is two to four weeks
> - L is one to two months
> - XL is more than two months
>
> This will provide a rough, high-level timeline for your project. You can revisit this frequently to understand how your original estimates change as part of your regular project management processes, such as sprint planning.

Finalize the Design Choices for the Cloud Data Lake

When it comes to a cloud data lake, there is a diverse set of options available, from architecture patterns, cloud providers, and specific services on the cloud. In this section, let's take a closer look at how to make these choices with the decision framework.

Picking your architecture

In "Design Considerations" on page 58, I walked you through an assessment of the various factors that go into deciding on a cloud data lake architecture. I encourage you to refresh your memory by reviewing Table 2-1.

The cost versus complexity comparison of the architectures shown in Figure 7-4 comes into play here as well.

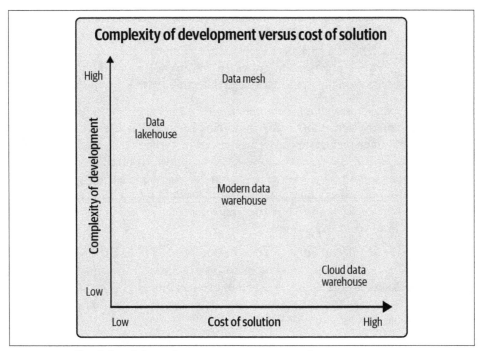

Figure 7-4. Cloud data lake architecture cost versus complexity

Now that you have refreshed your memory on these concepts, you can make an assessment of the architecture that is the right fit for you. I will add a few more factors for you to keep in mind:

Architectures could evolve over time
Depending on your discoveries during Phase 1, you can address your customer and business needs in an all-or-nothing or a hybrid fashion. As an example, if you have requirements from the marketing team to support data science scenarios, and the sales team wants to support dashboards for the quarterly sales projections, one option is to implement a modern data warehouse architecture where your data scientists leverage tools that directly operate on data in the data lake while your business analysts from the sales team consume the data and the dashboards from the data warehouse. Alternatively, you can start with this modern data warehouse and eventually migrate the data warehouse scenarios to run directly on the data lake, evolving into a lakehouse architecture.

Architectures can compose over one another
Cloud data lake architectures are not mutually exclusive and can compose on top of one another. For instance, most customers I have talked to have an existing data warehouse that serves their business needs. The most common first step is to introduce a cloud data lake, which essentially helps minimize the cost (by

storing past versions of the data) and supports new scenarios, such as machine learning. As a second step, the data warehouse moves to the cloud, either in the modern data lake or a lakehouse architecture, composing on top of this existing data lake. As your organization grows, so will the variety of the scenarios, and you can compose on top of the existing architectures with a data mesh.

Architectures span across multiple cloud providers
A note to always remember is the cloud data lake architecture does not enforce a unilateral implementation across a single set of components, enabling a multi-cloud or a hybrid cloud architecture. As an example, organizations that have an on-premises architecture have data analysts consuming their on-premises data warehouse. When they move to the cloud, they could start with a cloud data lake for data science scenarios while their business analysts continue to operate on premises in a hybrid architecture.

In summary, the architecture that you choose doesn't need to be constrained by your implementation choices. You choose your architecture based on your customer and business needs and have flexibility in actual implementation.

Picking your cloud provider

Once you've decided on an architecture, the next choice is to pick a cloud provider. Although there are multiple private cloud providers and hybrid cloud offerings, we'll focus on the most common and popular choices: the public cloud providers. The most popular cloud providers for cloud data lake services are AWS Lake Formation (*https://oreil.ly/-5Kz-*) that leverages Amazon S3 (*https://oreil.ly/XmNp3*), Azure Data Lake Storage (*https://oreil.ly/emSy9*), and cloud data lake offerings from Google Cloud (*https://oreil.ly/SF6m3*), composed of Google Cloud Storage (*https://oreil.ly/KgwbH*) and BigQuery (*https://oreil.ly/MBJWs*). The public cloud providers across AWS, Azure, and GCP have their own highly scalable distributed cloud data lake storage solutions, along with cloud native ingestion and orchestration services and managed data processing offerings that are compatible with open source offerings like Hadoop and Spark. These public cloud services have a healthy competition with one another on usability, price, and other data-related features, offering a rich set of services to cloud data lake customers.

To identify the right cloud services provider for you, there are a few factors to consider:

Cost of your solution
Identify the cloud services required to build your cloud data lake architecture, and ensure that the cost of the solution meets your budget.

Cloud service capabilities

> While the cloud service providers have highly comparable features, they also have some unique nuanced capabilities. As an example, AWS Lake Formation provides a simplified interface to get started and orchestrate your cloud data lake, and Azure Data Lake Storage offers a truly no-siloed data store that supports multiple protocols, including Network File System (NFS) version 3.

Integration with your other cloud services

> If you already have an implementation with a particular cloud provider, then that is the best starting point for your cloud data lake implementation. You could extend your current cloud implementation into the data services. As an example, if you already have a web application running on the cloud, your data platform could leverage ingesting logs or clickstream data from the web application to enables scenarios like customer dashboards or personalization features to your web application. This is a good starting point because you're starting on familiar terrain and extending an existing implementation.

The best way to assess the capabilities of the cloud providers is to do a PoC implementation of your scenarios. This will help you understand the best fit for your needs while also informing you about the cost profile of these solutions. Pick a PoC that best illustrates the needs of your customers. As an example, when Klodars Corporation is evaluating cloud data lakes, it can pick two of its highest-priority problems:

- The sales dashboards are taking a long time to refresh, disrupting the executive review meetings.
- The marketing team needs to understand how to best target its social media campaigns based on analysis of existing trends.

When Klodars did a PoC on the three cloud providers, it found that AWS Lake Formation offered the simplest implementation for its cloud data lake; Azure Data Lake Storage offered the lowest cost as well as interoperability with its on-premises systems with NFS v3 support; and Google BigQuery offered the fastest performance on both structured and unstructured data while scaling better than the data warehouse solutions on AWS and Azure. Given that Klodars's biggest pain point is around performance, it picked GCP for its cloud data lake implementation.

Decision points for data lake migrations

If you have an existing on-premises infrastructure (either data lake or data warehouse) that you would like to migrate to a cloud data lake architecture, then you have a few choices to make. These can be bucketed under three major design choices:

Lift and shift

In this design choice, you are preserving your existing design and primarily changing the hosting to the cloud. The advantage of this approach is it requires minimal refactoring of your code and components, so you can get going on the cloud sooner. Most public cloud providers like AWS, Azure, and GCP offer programs and automation optimized for most common lift-and-shift architectures. However, this does have a downside in that you will not be taking advantage of the native cloud capabilities and the key promise of the decoupled architecture of the cloud. In this scenario, you're most likely going to use IaaS and replicate your on-premises architecture on the cloud.

Replat and improve

In this design choice, you're still preserving your existing architecture and higher-level design; however, you will incorporate better scalability, reliability, and automation in your implementation, also referred to as *replat*. For example, you could take this opportunity to implement the technical debt that has been in your backlog for a long time, and you can take advantage of the features that public clouds offer to build better reliability, such as building in native failover.

Rip and replace

In this design choice, you will revisit the design from scratch and rearchitect/refactor your application to be cloud native. This essentially is equivalent to building your solutions to your business problems from scratch. This takes longer to implement but helps you take maximum advantage of the benefits the cloud offers. In this scenario, you can leverage the multitude of PaaS and IaaS offerings from the cloud provider to build your data lake solution.

Plan Your Cloud Data Lake Project Deliverables

The process of planning your cloud data lake deliverables can be broken down into three stages:

Ingest the raw data into the data lake

The first deliverable is to ingest data into your data lake. Set up scheduled ingest and orchestration jobs to ingest the relevant data. Inventory the datasets and frequency of the ingestion, and leverage that to guide your cloud data lake ingestion. As an example, Klodars Corporation's top pain points are around sales dashboards performance and marketing data science scenarios. It prioritizes ingestion of the sales data from its on-premises operational databases on a daily basis, and data from social media feeds into its cloud data lake on a weekly basis given the exploratory nature of the analytics. It also prepares these datasets by deduping and fixing any validation errors. It optimizes the formats by converting them into an optimal data format like Apache Parquet.

High-value data processing

   The next deliverable to plan is the data processing to generate high-value data for analysis from the raw and the curated datasets. As an example, Klodars Corporation will plan the data processing required for preparing its sales dashboards and the data processing on social media trends required for its marketing campaigns. Klodars leverages Apache Spark for both of these data processing jobs and continues to optimize its performance with the various techniques discussed in Chapter 5.

Integrate with other systems

   The final deliverable to plan is integrating the high-value activities with other systems, such as your cloud data warehouses, and any other applications as needed. These could be other cloud services or applications that run in your on-premises systems.

Once you have an initial version of the design and the project plan, revisit the customer and business requirements that you finalized at the end of Phase 1, and ensure that your design and timelines meet these requirements. If not, tune your design and implementation as appropriate. In addition, you may have discovered additional customer or business requirements. In this case, ensure that you tune Phase 1 to reflect the reprioritization in light of these discoveries. At the end of Phase 2, make sure that you have high confidence in the prioritized requirements and that the architecture and design will sustain you for at least the next one to two years.

Involving Your Customers and Business Leaders

Based on my experience, a best practice I recommend is to share your Phase 1 and Phase 2 deliverables with your customers and business leaders to get their early input and feedback. Focus your communications on what matters to them. As an example, instead of saying, "We will complete ingest by end of May 2022," you could say, "The sales datasets will be available in the cloud data lake storage by the end of May 2022. You can access these datasets by filing a request to the data platform team using this form." Also involve a subset of your customers in validating your deliverables early, during the intermittent milestones. I recommend selecting customers in two categories: customers who are highly motivated to test the data lake and customers who have the hardest requirements that could pose risks and surprises. Having a healthy mix of these two segments will help you derisk your deliverables early on.

Phase 3 of Decision Framework: Implement

When you exit Phase 2, you have finalized the technical architecture and design, and you have a project plan ready with a final plan and scope. In Phase 3, the metaphorical rubber hits the road, and you will be executing against the timelines. A good barometer of a high-confidence Phase 1 and Phase 2 is that your implementation phase runs smoothly without any major surprises or changes. Having said that, stay adaptable so you can fine-tune your plan based on the next level of discoveries.

In Phase 3, in addition to working on meeting the customer deliverables, the main thing you need to think about is ensuring that you have the basic foundation in place to manage your cloud data lake as it scales and grows. We discussed the design considerations for the cloud data lake implementation at length in Chapter 3. As a refresher, the three key areas of focus here are as follows:

Data organization
> Data follows a natural lifecycle of being ingested in its raw natural state, cleaned and prepared for further processing, and further curated with aggregations or filtering to generate high-value density data for consumption. In addition, a segment of your customers, such as data scientists, will want to bring in their own datasets for doing their analysis. Ensure that you have an organization mechanism incorporated into your data lake based on who accesses the data and how, and be sure to manage policies such as data retention.

Data governance
> The ultimate goal of data governance is to build trust in your data, which is especially important considering the number of critical business decisions that are made based on data. As the usage of data in your data lake grows and scales, data governance must meet the following requirements:
>
> - Your data lake implementation meets the policies or compliance requirements defined by your data officers.
> - The datasets that are generated by the data producers are discoverable for consumption by the data consumers.
> - The data platform team can offer assurances on data quality to the data producers, consumers, and data officers, building trust in the data.

Data lake cost management
> One of the highest-value propositions of a cloud data lake architecture is supporting a large variety of use cases around data at a lower cost. However, this lower cost relies on the fact that the architecture and implementation are designed with a cloud architecture in mind. This requires a basic understanding of the cost drivers of your data lake, which are the *storage costs*, *compute costs*, *networking costs*, and *software and license costs*. Understanding these cost drivers and implementing a design that follows an optimal cost profile while meeting the requirements are key to managing the costs of the data lake.

I recommend using Chapter 3 as a reference for these three focus areas as part of your cloud data lake implementation. The amount of investment in these areas largely depends on the maturity of your organization and the expected scale of growth over the next two years. Table 7-1 list some good rules of thumb to follow depending on the scale of your data lake implementation.

Table 7-1. Cloud data lake implementation considerations depending on the scale of your organization

Area of investment	Reference	Small-scale data lake (largely controlled by the data platform team end to end)	Large-scale data lake (data platform team is running into limits or the use cases are highly variegated and hard for the data team to keep track of)
Data organization	"Organizing Data in Your Data Lake" on page 73	Organize your cloud data lake storage into zones using the storage organization mechanisms.	Organize your cloud data lake storage into zones. Organize your compute processing clusters in a way that segments critical data pipelines from noncritical exploratory data usage.
Data governance: data classification	"Data Classification" on page 81	Manual or semiautomated would suffice; plan for automated classification.	Automated data classification is a hard requirement; the manual or semiautomated classification does not scale.
Data governance: data discovery	"Metadata Management, Data Catalog, and Data Sharing" on page 82	Publish the metadata in a metastore or a data catalog offering that is not too expensive. Data sharing is useful if you share your datasets with other organizations.	Invest in a self-serve data catalog that can be used by data producers; data sharing will largely help with the self-serve approach.
Data governance: data access management	"Data Access Management" on page 83	Implement storage-, compute-, and network-level access policies. Data-access-policy tools are nice to have but not a hard requirement.	Data access tools at the cross-component level are a worthy investment that reduces the load on the data team. Implement complex policies based on the data classification scales to meet compliance requirements. In some cases, you can lock down access at the compute, storage, and network levels to the bare minimum and leverage these data access policies for end-to-end data management.
Data governance: data quality and observability	"Data Quality and Observability" on page 85	Define SLAs and SLOs for your critical datasets and jobs; monitoring could be semi-automated to start.	Invest in data quality and data observability solutions to be able to scale to the diverse use cases running on your data lake.
Data lake cost management	"Manage Data Lake Costs" on page 89	Understand every line in your cloud data lake bill to avoid surprises. Implement data retention policies and tiered storage to optimize data lake storage costs.	In addition to the small-scale data lake practices, implement quotas for consumption across your departments to ensure there are no surprises.

At the end of Phase 3, the goal is to have a timely launch with a complete set of features, while also ensuring that the data platform team is set up for smooth operation of the data lake.

Phase 4 of Decision Framework: Operationalize

When you build and ship software, whether a website or a mobile application or a software application, the primary focus is on code, and any change in requirements and functionality can be accomplished by changing the code. However, in the development of data, changes in code, data, or configurations can alter the behavior of the consumption patterns.

Operationalizing the data lake involves the following components:

Managing new requirements or change requests
> You can almost be certain that the number of use cases that run on your data lake will continue to grow, and it's only a matter of time before you will get new requests. You can use a process similar to Phase 1 to triage and debug the requirements.

Troubleshooting and debugging
> As with a software product, ensure that you have a process and workflow for incident management. It is a best practice to have an on-call support system for your data platform similar to support for a software system. The SLAs, SLOs, and SLIs you set for your data platform are critical to prioritizing the level of engagement for customer issues. I also recommend that you track the various incidents and the associated root causes to ensure that you can identify the areas where technical debt is built and address them systematically. These could involve performance tuning or identifying scale bottlenecks, among other areas. Chapter 4 and Chapter 5 provide more context and information on the approaches to tuning your cloud data lake for scale and performance.

Summary

In the first six chapters, I went through the various aspects of designing, building, and implementing a cloud data lake solution. In this chapter, I have put all of these learnings together to show you how to apply these concepts as you build your cloud data lake solution. I introduced a four-step framework of assess, define, implement, and operationalize in describing these concepts. You can use this framework as is or customize it as you see fit. My strong recommendation is that you take the time to assess your business and customer requirements and use those to guide your design and implementation. The due diligence you do in earlier phases ensures a smoother operation. Finally, expect new discoveries at every stage, so go back to the output of your previous phases and tune it as you see fit.

CHAPTER 8

Six Lessons for a Data Informed Future

It's amazing how a little tomorrow can make up for a whole lot of yesterday.

—John Guare

The promise of a cloud data lake architecture lies in the boundless diversity of scenarios that it enables. In the previous chapters, we've focused on the most commonly used patterns of data processing with Spark- and Hadoop-flavored technologies. Other aspects—such as real-time stream processing, which generates quick insights on real-time data, and advanced analytics scenarios, which build smart applications on the data lake—are gaining fast adoption. One thing that all the concepts and frameworks we covered in the previous chapters have in common is that at every juncture in the design or implementation of the cloud data lake, choices are available to you, and each choice comes with trade-offs on cost, complexity, and flexibility. As you make these decisions when designing your cloud data lake, it's only natural to have the following questions:

- How do I know I made the right choice?
- As my organization grows and so do the scenarios on my data lake, how do I iterate and drive transformation?
- How do I ensure that my organization can be agile to gather and address the next set of requirements?
- How do I think about a global strategy and stay ahead of the needs of my organization?

In this chapter, I leverage the format of lessons learned to provide a structure for you to think about the technical, cultural, and organizational decisions that will help you realize the value of data for your organization.

Lesson 1: Focus on the How and When, Not the If and Why, When It Comes to Cloud Data Lakes

As of April 2022, about five million people use the internet every day, and this number continues to grow at an annual rate of 4%. With the advent of social media, more connected devices like smart appliances, and the acceleration of remote work during the COVID-19 pandemic, data has become as omnipresent as it can get. It is only natural that this proliferation of data paves the way for intelligent decision making by organizations. According to the State of Data Practice study conducted by Molecula (*https://oreil.ly/ODOff*), which was based on interviews with 300 data practitioners across various industries, there was an overwhelming acknowledgment of the value of data to their organizations. According to this survey, 96% of the respondents agreed that their organizations are using data effectively, and 70% indicated that companies without a data strategy would go out of business.

This survey not only highlights the criticality of data to running and operating businesses but also gives a clear signal of the risk associated with not investing in data. In the same survey, only 22% of the respondents indicated that they have deployed machine learning models in production within the past two years, and only 2% indicated that they have deployed machine learning models in production within the past five years. This is not surprising given the complexities associated with these advanced analytics scenarios.

What does this mean for your organization? As I have indicated many times before, a cloud data lake strategy is critical to your organization—it is not a question of if or why you need a cloud data lake. However, depending on the skill sets and maturity of your organization, you can decide how far you would like to go.

If there is one thing I strongly recommend, it is to invest in a cloud data lake and start collecting and processing data that you believe is useful to your organization today. This could be your database backups, social media feeds, or data from other LOB systems such as sales or marketing dashboards. There are well-understood patterns that you can also start implementing, such as BI scenarios around generating dashboards on how your organization is performing. Again, betting on the cloud is an important part of this strategy because the cloud offers a set of off-the-shelf services that help you get started while providing flexibility of choices and an elastic infrastructure to support your growth. This gets you to the initial part of your data journey, where you derive insights on how your organization is performing. At the same time, depending on the requirements of your organization, you can identify a few key bets based on customer needs to prototype and implement more advanced scenarios—this takes both organizational and cultural transformation in the right direction. Find your highly motivated customers and work with them.

The journey of a thousand miles begins with a single step. Once you take that first step, it is only a matter of time before you see yourself sprinting ahead.

Lesson 2: With Great Power Comes Great Responsibility—Data Is No Exception

With the great power and diversity of scenarios that data brings to your organization, one important aspect for you to consider is managing the data end to end in a responsible fashion, adhering to ethical business practices and ensuring fairness and equitable experiences for your customers.

Let's see this with an example. With the data strategy and a cloud data lake in place, Klodars Corporation leverages social media trends and correlates them with its sales and customer data to understand the consumption patterns. It identifies that customers between ages 30 and 45 tend to click on campaigns and ads in social media to buy umbrellas and rain gear from its websites. This helps its marketing department target campaigns and offer discounts and promotions to customers of this age group. While this helps the business, Klodars inadvertently optimizes its business for customers in this age group, potentially having the side effect of marginalizing older customers. One of the reasons older customers did not buy from the website could be because they were not using social media as actively as the other demographics, which ended up as a disadvantage for the company. In the longer term, this also affects the business because once it saturates the market for ages 30–45, Klodars doesn't have a way to expand.

Although this is an example I crafted to illustrate the issue of having a responsible data strategy, it is not far from reality. According to the *Washington Post* article "Racial Bias in a Medical Algorithm Favors White Patients Over Sicker Black Patients," (*https://oreil.ly/OLwMO*) a health services provider company named Optum leveraged data to understand what segment of patients would benefit from extra medical care. Unfortunately, the company is now under investigation because its algorithm allegedly undermined the health needs of Black patients due to the bias in the datasets toward a certain segment of our population.

To ensure that you start with the right set of governance, security, and ethical practices in your cloud data lake strategy, here are some of the practices you can put in place:

Include and consult the experts in your organization to proactively identify data risks
> You most likely have a regulatory body in your organization for other parts of your business; this could be your legal department, compliance organization, or any regulatory affairs department. Involve them early, ensure that you understand the risks and best practices associated with data, and incorporate these into your data lake design and implementation. Review your data strategy with

your regulatory team and incorporate their feedback. If they are not aware of data-related risks and best practices, ensure that they follow up with industry experts and articles to give you the right level of advice.

Provide transparency to your customers, and respect their privacy
When you collect customer data, make sure you are transparent with them about what data you will collect and what you will use it for. Further, ensure that you respect their privacy and provide a way for them to give consent to sharing their data. Make sure your data collection, storage, and processing meet privacy and compliance policies. Some examples of these policies are GDPR (*https://gdpr-info.eu*) and CCPA (*https://oreil.ly/lHqLE*). For a complete list, talk to your organizational experts. It's also important that you either scrub PII as part of your data processing or, if you store it for a specific reason, ask for consent explicitly to protect consumer privacy and security in your implementation.

Do your best to identify, anticipate, and avoid inequitable or unfair outcomes
As your data estate grows and you leverage advanced machine learning techniques more, it becomes more difficult to spot the inequitable outcomes of your algorithms, such as the example with Optum we discussed previously. Further, any software comes with bugs, and you definitely want to make sure that the bugs don't result in unpleasant or unfair outcomes for your customers, especially when their data is involved. As part of your data strategy or requirements definitions, involve your experts to add specific requirements for fairness and ethics when it comes to data. Especially if you're using AI in your solutions, the bias in data and your algorithms could have unintended side effects, making investment in ethics and fairness all the more important. Courses such as AI Ethics Global Perspectives (*https://aiethicscourse.org*) can help you build more awareness and knowledge in this area. Treat these requirements as a high priority in your implementation. At the end of the day, building trust in your data lays a strong foundation for building customer trust in your organization.

Ensure that you have both proactive and reactive frameworks for data-related issues
In addition to proactively identifying and designing these best practices in your data lake strategy, it is important for you to have the ability to react to incidents quickly. Similar to how you would design for supporting code after shipping, ensure that you have guardrails and controls in place to mitigate data issues. Invest in data observability, identify SLAs and SLOs for your data, and monitor them.

In summary, ensure that you are responsible, ethical, and fair in your data strategy and cloud data lake implementation. In addition, talk to your cloud providers and your ISVs about their fair practices. The more proactive you are in considering and prioritizing these aspects, the better set up you will be for a smoother implementation and operationalization.

Lesson 3: Customers Lead Technology, Not the Other Way Around

Big data and analytics are exciting areas for technologists. The problems are very open ended, and there are ample opportunities to innovate in this space. The Apache Software Foundation (*https://projects.apache.org*) has 56 projects in the big data technologies category, and every time I attend a data conference, I continue to be impressed by the growing number of vendors holding booths, both in person and virtually. When it comes to what matters to you and your organization, one trap you want to avoid is being lured by the promise of specific technologies and later figuring out that they are not in the critical path of what really matters to your customers and your business. Always start with scoping and prioritizing your business and customer needs, and find the technology that is a good fit for your needs.

As an example, Klodars Corporation has identified two key scenarios for its cloud data lake implementation: powering the executive sales dashboards and leveraging social media feeds to build targeted marketing campaigns. Alice, who heads the data platform team, realizes that there is a real-time social media feed streaming service that would provide live trends on social media. While this is very exciting for Alice, she talks to the data scientists and marketing team and realizes that it is not critical for them to have live trends. Instead, they want a way to import social media feeds on a daily basis to analyze and understand longer-term trends over weeks. Although this service offers innovative technology, it is not critical for her business needs, and she does not prioritize it immediately.

Or consider a real-life analogy, as illustrated in Figure 8-1: when you want to buy furniture, you wouldn't go to a store and ask for craftspeople with mad skills using the power saw or the drill; you want to see a table for your study or your dining room. Similarly, when you implement your data lake, you always start with your requirements, as we saw in "Phase 1 of Decision Framework: Assess" on page 175. Anytime you evaluate a technology, be it a service or a service provider, ensure that you center the conversations on your requirements and evaluate the technology in terms of its cost and complexity for you. Technology is very transient and potentially gets outdated over time; what matters is the durability of the scenarios that run on top of your data lake.

Figure 8-1. Customer requirements versus technologies

Lesson 4: Change Is Inevitable, so Be Prepared

As a corollary to "Lesson 3: Customers Lead Technology, Not the Other Way Around" on page 195, in the spirit of leading with customers and your business requirements, be adaptable to change because it's inevitable. Now, now, when I say change, I don't necessarily mean churn. *Churn* refers to rapidly changing the activities and your plan when they are in flux—this is disruptive to your organization and slows your progress. *Change* refers to an inevitable movement in requirements and helps you plan for and execute this movement thoughtfully.

When it comes to data lakes, some things usually stay constant: the storage and processing patterns. Change could come in any of the following ways:

Adding new components and processing or consumption patterns to respond to new requirements

As an example, Klodars Corporation implemented a modern data warehouse architecture to support the sales dashboards for business analysts and the targeted marketing campaign work for the data scientists. New requirements were identified to add product recommendations as customers are shopping on the website, so Klodars added a real-time processing pipeline that feeds in customer clickstream data from its websites to serve relevant recommendations.

Optimizing existing architecture for better cost or performance

As an example, Klodars Corporation ingested backups of its databases to power its sales dashboards. However, it found that the growing size of the backups increased the cost of the data lake storage over time. In addition, there were common patterns such as identifying sales data by regions, customer segments, and salespeople. Klodars implemented optimizations to data storage by converting these database formats to Apache Iceberg, which offered lower costs due to the high degree of compression as well as faster performance for queries on data in the data lake with the columnar format.

Some of these changes are additive and don't affect existing use cases. However, there are some instances where your changes are disruptive. Ensure that the disruptive changes are managed appropriately, set customer expectations up front, and offer a lower-barrier path to their transition. In cases where you are performing these transitions, ensure that you are supporting the existing design, and provide ample time for your customers to move to the new design.

Lesson 5: Build Empathy and Prioritize Ruthlessly

It's true that data and data strategy are critical to the organization; however, it's also true that data by itself is a means to the end of business or customer impact unless you're a provider of data or data-related services. As an example, if you're in the manufacturing industry, data can help with critical use cases like predictive maintenance or supply chain optimizations. However, the impact of the data platform itself is realized through reduced failure rates on the devices or fewer items in the inventory, which is the business language. As a result, it's fair to assume that it is key for the data platform team to drive efficiencies and optimize its own operations. As far as my personal experience goes, I've often seen the data platform be a lean organization where the demands are always higher than what the team can support at a given time.

It's important for the data platform team to be set up for success by ensuring that the lean team can scale to growing customer needs. At the same time, do ensure that at every point in time you are operating with empathy for the customer. You are the data experts; your customers have other areas of expertise, and data expertise should not be a requirement for them. In your investments, prioritize for end-to-end customer experiences that are seamless, and err on the side of saying no rather than offering a poorly implemented or half-baked solution.

Let me take a fictitious example to illustrate this point. Klodars Corporation has a data platform team that needs to serve sales, marketing, and the rain gear product line as well as a recent acquisition of a winter gear business. So the team implements a data mesh architecture and offers blueprints for a data lake domain that these customers can implement with a self-serve model. The blueprint includes templates to provision cloud resources required for the data lake, and the customers can choose the cloud services. However, the sales, marketing, and rain gear teams do not have enough information on whether they need to choose a data lake alone or a data lake and data warehouse. So the sales and marketing teams approach the data platform team with questions. But the rain gear product team chooses a data lake alone, when its need is to build a warehouse for its supply chain inventory. This ends up creating dissatisfaction for the customers while increasing the load for the data platform team, who has to react to their questions and issues.

An alternative path for the data platform team would be to do an end-to-end implementation with the sales and marketing team while deprioritizing the use cases for the time being for the other customers. Based on the learnings from this implementation, the data platform team can evaluate the readiness for a self-serve architecture with a data mesh and roll it out more broadly.

In summary, setting expectations up front is more optimal than setting the customer up for disappointment later. Be transparent and clear about your prioritizations, and set expectations with your customers about when you'll be able to serve them.

Lesson 6: Big Impact Does Not Happen Overnight

Finally, this is probably more of a life lesson that also applies to data lake architectures. The culmination of big impact has many steps and lessons and failures behind it. Cloud data lake architectures offer great promise, but they also require a lot of learning and iterations before you get them right. As an example, Apache Iceberg (*https://iceberg.apache.org*), a very popular open source technology that supports the lakehouse pattern today, had humble beginnings in Netflix, which started with an implementation to overcome the then-shortcomings of Amazon S3 object storage. The Netflix team believed in the power of data for its organization and thoughtfully implemented Apache Iceberg to serve its customers with high-quality data with strong guarantees on top of lower-cost object storage. As they say, the rest is history, and you can learn more about this by revisiting "Apache Iceberg" on page 157.

Plan for customer impact, and prepare to learn and fine-tune as you progress. Make choices based on the impact they offer to customers, and stay consistent in your implementation while keeping open-minded for learnings. Especially if you are an early adopter of a technology, you can help develop the technology with the provider and thus get ample support from the technology provider in return. Similarly, identify highly motivated early adopters within your customer base and offer to develop your solution with them. Celebrate your successes together, and share your credits.

Summary

I was brainstorming with my editors on various ways to end this book, and I thought it fitting that I end with a set of six lessons that you can apply regardless of where you're in your data lake journey. First and foremost, huge kudos to you for taking this step, and remember that you're already on your path to innovating your business—it is only a matter of time before things fall into place. Data is the future, and cloud is where this future is happening as we speak. We're all part of defining this future by investing in cloud data lakes.

The technologies and cloud offerings themselves have seen rapid improvements over time, and these changes can be overwhelming. I personally always start with the basics of what is important to a project and why it is important, and I have structured my book to build this fundamental framework that can be leveraged in spite of the technologies used. To keep on top of the various technologies, I recommend that you watch the conferences from data vendors and public cloud providers to stay abreast of trends. There are also a ton of resources available for various technologies on podcasts and YouTube. I would especially recommend that, in addition to watching the sessions from the technology builders, you watch the customer sessions on what problems they solved, which will give you great ideas. Data+AI Summit (*https://oreil.ly/AN7zr*) is one of my favorite conferences, and the sessions are available on demand for your viewing.

We're at that point where this book has reached its natural conclusion, and I thank you for being a great audience. I'm really excited to learn more about where your cloud data lake journey takes you. If you want to share your experiences or ask a question, or you want to brainstorm about what is a good choice for you, reach out to me, and I'll be more than happy to chat more. I'm on Twitter as @rukmanigopalan (*https://mobile.twitter.com/rukmanigopalan*), and you can find me on LinkedIn at *https://www.linkedin.com/in/rukmanig*.

Cloud Data Lake Decision Framework Template

In this section, I'll provide a template that you can use to plan your cloud data lake solution. You can customize this template as needed based on your specific scenarios or customers. I recommend that you plan at least over a one- to two-year horizon to ensure that your cloud data lake design is sustainable before you have to make drastic changes.

Phase 1: Assess Framework

Target 60%–70% accuracy and completeness

The objective of this phase is to define and prioritize the requirements for the cloud data lake that will drive your architecture and implementation decisions. In this phase, the data engineering team needs to identify the requirements based on two key aspects: customer requirements and business drivers. I strongly recommend doing your due diligence in the assess phase, which will set you up for smooth planning and execution of the subsequent phases.

Use Table A-1 to record the findings from your stakeholder interviews.

Table A-1. Inventory of problems and requirements

Customer	Problem	Severity of problem	Helpfulness of data lake	How cloud data lake can help
		High/Medium/Low	High/Medium/Low	
		High/Medium/Low	High/Medium/Low	
		High/Medium/Low	High/Medium/Low	
		High/Medium/Low	High/Medium/Low	
		High/Medium/Low	High/Medium/Low	
		High/Medium/Low	High/Medium/Low	

Once you have defined your requirements, prioritize them against the business drivers, and use Table A-2 to prioritize the requirements of your cloud data lake.

Table A-2. Requirements for your cloud data lake

Priority	Requirement
High/Medium/Low	
High/Medium/Low	
High/Medium/Low	

Priority	Requirement
High/Medium/Low	
High/Medium/Low	
High/Medium/Low	

Phase 2: Define Framework

Target 80%–90% accuracy and completeness

In this phase, you'll use the prioritized list of requirements defined in Phase 1 to define and plan the technical components. The key objective of this phase is to complete the technical design and project plan that are required to meet the customer and business requirements determined in the Assess phase. This plan then helps scope the time and resource requirements for the project.

Table A-3 captures the design considerations and decisions of the various aspects of your cloud data lake design and implementation.

Table A-3. Design decisions for the cloud data lake

Design area	Considerations	Reference	Finalized choice
Cloud data lake architecture	Cost requirements: Complexity considerations: Variety of scenarios: Skill set of teams:	"Design Considerations" on page 58	Architecture choice:
Cloud provider	Cost requirements: Performance requirements: Other applications and services considerations:	"Cloud Computing Fundamentals" on page 8	Finalized choice of cloud provider:

Design area	Considerations	Reference	Finalized choice
Cloud services	Available IaaS options: Available PaaS options: Available SaaS options: Proof-of-concept evaluations:	"Cloud Computing Fundamentals" on page 8	Finalized choices:

Once you finalize the design choices and the technical components of your cloud data lake, you will put together the project plan by identifying the deliverables of your cloud data lake implementation.

Planning the Cloud Data Lake Deliverables

In Table A-4, you can record various datasets that need to be ingested into the cloud data lake.

Table A-4. Data ingestion deliverables

Dataset to be ingested	Frequency	Data prep requirements	Data size

Dataset to be ingested	Frequency	Data prep requirements	Data size

In Table A-5, you can record the data processing requirements, which list the data preparation and data curation transformations and the finalized choices of what data processing technology (as an example, Spark or Hadoop) and tooling (for instance, run Spark on a VM, use a Databricks cluster) will be used.

Table A-5. Data processing deliverables

Input datasets	Output datasets	Data processing tool	Requirements (configurations, VMs required, etc.)

Input datasets	Output datasets	Data processing tool	Requirements (configurations, VMs required, etc.)

In Table A-6, you can track the various systems that your cloud data lake will integrate. This is in effect the output of your data lake that your customers will use.

Table A-6. Data integration deliverables

System (dashboards, on-premises systems, other cloud systems)	Datasets	Data integration tool	Requirements (configurations, VMs required, etc.)	Pilot customers signed up for validation

Phase 3: Implement Framework

Target 100% accuracy and completeness

You can use Table A-7 to record and track the data organization within your data lake.

Table A-7. Data lake organization planning

Zone (raw/enriched/curated/workspace)	Dataset	Access type (read/write)	Audience	Retention period for data

Once you have identified your data assets, you can use Table A-8 to record and track the stakeholders who interact with your datasets and how these datasets can be discovered and managed.

Table A-8. Data governance tracking

Data producers	Datasets	SLAs/SLOs	Published in catalog (Yes/No/ Planned)	Special policies based on classification	Retention period for data	Data sharing policies

Data producers	Datasets	SLAs/SLOs	Published in catalog (Yes/No/ Planned)	Special policies based on classification	Retention period for data	Data sharing policies

In Table A-9, I provide a framework for you to track and understand the various cost drivers for your data lake and how you can work on optimizing your costs.

Table A-9. Data lake cost management

Data lake environment (development/ testing/pre- production/ production)	SLAs and SLOs	Data storage requirements	Data compute requirements	Data networking requirements
		Redundancy: Durability (versioning, etc.): Tiering policies: Default retention policies:	Cluster configurations for scheduled jobs: Cluster configurations for ad hoc jobs: Caching: Software licensing:	Network bandwidth from on premises: Cross-region data access requirements: Data egress out-of-region requirements:

Data lake environment (development/ testing/pre-production/ production)	SLAs and SLOs	Data storage requirements	Data compute requirements	Data networking requirements
		Redundancy: Durability (versioning, etc.): Tiering policies: Default retention policies:	Cluster configurations for scheduled jobs: Cluster configurations for ad hoc jobs: Caching: Software licensing:	Network bandwidth from on premises: Cross-region data access requirements: Data egress out-of-region requirements:
		Redundancy: Durability (versioning, etc.): Tiering policies: Default retention policies:	Cluster configurations for scheduled jobs: Cluster configurations for ad hoc jobs: Caching: Software licensing:	Network bandwidth from on premises: Cross-region data access requirements: Data egress out-of-region requirements:
		Redundancy: Durability (versioning, etc.): Tiering policies: Default retention policies:	Cluster configurations for scheduled jobs: Cluster configurations for ad hoc jobs: Caching: Software licensing:	Network bandwidth from on premises: Cross-region data access requirements: Data egress out-of-region requirements:
		Redundancy: Durability (versioning, etc.): Tiering policies: Default retention policies:	Cluster configurations for scheduled jobs: Cluster configurations for ad hoc jobs: Caching: Software licensing:	Network bandwidth from on premises: Cross-region data access requirements: Data egress out-of-region requirements:

Data lake environment (development/ testing/pre- production/ production)	SLAs and SLOs	Data storage requirements	Data compute requirements	Data networking requirements
		Redundancy: Durability (versioning, etc.): Tiering policies: Default retention policies:	Cluster configurations for scheduled jobs: Cluster configurations for ad hoc jobs: Caching: Software licensing:	Network bandwidth from on premises: Cross-region data access requirements: Data egress out-of-region requirements:
		Redundancy: Durability (versioning, etc.): Tiering policies: Default retention policies:	Cluster configurations for scheduled jobs: Cluster configurations for ad hoc jobs: Caching: Software licensing:	Network bandwidth from on premises: Cross-region data access requirements: Data egress out-of-region requirements:
		Redundancy: Durability (versioning, etc.): Tiering policies: Default retention policies:	Cluster configurations for scheduled jobs: Cluster configurations for ad hoc jobs: Caching: Software licensing:	Network bandwidth from on premises: Cross-region data access requirements: Data egress out-of-region requirements:

Finally, as prepared as we are, it is important to always be ready when things go wrong. You can use Table A-10 to understand what went wrong when you have incidents and how to mitigate these issues as well as to plan improvements to reduce the technical debt to minimize future occurrences.

Table A-10. Incident tracking

Incident	Type of problem (new data/new features/technical debt)	Affected customers	Severity of problem	Description of the work to be done	Timelines for requirement
	New data/new features/technical debt		High/ Medium/Low		
	New data/new features/technical debt		High/ Medium/Low		
	New data/new features/technical debt		High/ Medium/Low		
	New data/new features/technical debt		High/ Medium/Low		
	New data/new features/technical debt		High/ Medium/Low		
	New data/new features/technical debt		High/ Medium/Low		

Index

A

access management for data, 83
  Klodars Corporation, 87
ACID (atomicity, consistency, isolation, durability) compliance
  data warehouses ensuring, 42
  Delta Lake enabling, 154
Amazon Athena, 44
Amazon Kinesis, 33
Amazon Macie, 82
Amazon Redshift, 34
  Redshift Spectrum and lake houses, 40
Amazon S3 (Simple Storage Service), 26
  buckets for organizing data zones, 78
  data lake storage, 26, 184
  data lakehouse implementation, 44
Amazon Web Services (see AWS)
analytics engines for big data, 28-33
  Apache Hadoop, 29-31
  Apache Spark, 31
  data warehouse architecture, 36
  MapReduce, 28
  real-time stream processing, 32
Apache Airflow, 129
Apache Atlas, 87
Apache Flink, 33
Apache Hadoop, 29-31
  Apache Hive table SQL-like queries, 158
  data lakehouse data format, 46
  data processing engine, 105, 108
  selecting which to use, 30
Apache Hive tables, 158
Apache Hudi, 162-168
  about, 162-167

data lake technology, 44
file format, 164-167
incremental modifications, 163
managed platform built on, 168
open data format, 44, 164
  Apache Parquet architecture, 139
real-time insights, 164
strengths of, 47, 167
upserts, 163
when to use, 167
why founded, 163
Apache Iceberg, 157-162
  about, 157-161
  data lake technology, 44
  data partition optimization, 162
  file structure, 159-161
  open data format, 28, 44, 117
    Apache Parquet architecture, 139, 159
  scan planning, 162
  schema evolution, 162
  snapshot isolation, 162
  strengths of, 47, 161
  time travel, 162
  when to use, 161
  why founded, 157-159
Apache Kafka, 33, 38
Apache Nutch, 29
Apache ORC, 159
Apache Parquet
  about, 135
    video online explaining, 139
  about data lakehouse data format, 46
  Apache Spark efficiency, 110, 117
  costs lowered by, 139

snapshot isolation in Apache Iceberg, 162
Snowflake Data Cloud, 35, 69
software as a service (see SaaS)
Spark (see Apache Spark)
SQL
    Apache Hadoop and Apache Hive tables, 158
    data lakehouse data format, 45
    data warehouse optimization, 43
    Delta Lake queries on data lake, 47, 156
Starbucks data uses, 2
state management in real-time stream processing, 33
storage resources in scalability, 103, 116
streaming data
    Apache Hudi, 139, 164
    data ingestion by Apache Kafka, 33, 38
    real-time stream processing, 32
    velocity of big data, 5
structured data
    data categories for big data processing, 23
    data warehouses, 6
    legacy data systems, 13
subscription-based billing for cloud services, 11, 71

T

tabular data
    columnar format of data, 46
        Apache Hudi, 164
        Apache Iceberg via metadata, 162
        Apache Parquet, 135-139
        Apache Spark efficiency, 110
        Delta Lake, 155
    compute engine for data lakehouse, 47
    data lake unstructured data as, 44
    data partitioning, 141
    data prep after ingestion, 73, 75, 108
    open data formats
        about need for, 149
        why tabular data, 150-151
    schema specifications or descriptions, 154
TCO (total cost of ownership), 10, 43, 89
terminology of cloud computing, 8-10
throughput in performance measurement, 119
tiered storage, 26
time involved in implementation, 67, 181
    timelines for cloud data lake, 182
total cost of ownership (TCO), 10, 43, 89

tracking the lineage of the data, 79
transactions
    ACID compliance of data warehouses, 42
    transaction costs, 92
        strategies for, 95
troubleshooting cloud data lakes, 190

U

Uber (see Apache Hudi)
unstructured data
    data categories for big data processing, 25
    data lake ability to handle, 43
        defining the data, 44-47
    data warehouses supporting, 6, 51
upserts of Apache Hudi, 163
use cases (see Klodars Corporation (example company))

V

value of data in big data
    about, 7
    benefits of cloud data lake architecture, 15, 37
    cost of data warehouses versus lakes, 6, 37
    importance of data, 1, 169
    responsibly managing data, 193-194
    risks of not investing in data, 192
variability of big data
    about, 6
    benefits of cloud data lake architecture, 15, 37
variety in big data
    about, 5
    benefits of cloud data lake architecture, 15, 21, 37
    meaning of, 23-25
velocity of big data
    about, 5
    real-time stream processing, 32
        (see also streaming data)
veracity of big data
    about, 6
    ACID compliance
        data warehouses, 42
        Delta Lake, 154
    challenges of modern data warehouse, 40
vertical scaling, 116
volume of big data
    about, 4

data lake versus data warehouse, 4, 37
  scalability, 4
Vorwerck, Molly, 85

About the Author

Rukmani Gopalan is a product management leader who has worked on data infrastructure and platforms at Microsoft and other startups. Her goal is to educate data architects and data developers about the various aspects of building cloud data lake platforms. She believes that building a strong conceptual understanding of big data processing on the cloud leads to robust implementation of the data platform, thereby yielding transformational insights for the organization. She lives in Redmond, Washington, and enjoys exploring the Pacific Northwest, one conversation and cup of coffee at a time.

Colophon

The animal on the cover of *The Cloud Data Lake* is a fork-tailed storm-petrel (*Hydrates furcates*). They are silvery-blue colored seabirds. Their upper body is lighter than their underparts. True to their name, they have a forked tail. They also have a steep, gray forehead with a dark mask around their eyes and a small bill.

Fork-tailed storm-petrels have an expansive range across the cold waters of the Northern Pacific Ocean from Japan to California. They prefer to nest on islands that are hilly with good cover from grass and shrubs and are often found not far from shore. They are most commonly found off the shore of southern Alaska.

One special trait of this bird is that it has an amazing sense of smell and is therefore capable of tracking down food from many miles away. It also helps that one of their preferred meals is oily fat from wounded or dead animals that they skim off the surface of the water. Additionally, they eat fish, crustaceans, and zooplankton.

Because they have such a large territory and their population isn't decreasing, they are considered a species of least concern on endangered lists. Many of the animals on O'Reilly covers are endangered; all of them are important to the world.

The cover illustration is by Karen Montgomery, based on an antique line engraving from *British Birds*. The cover fonts are Gilroy Semibold and Guardian Sans. The text font is Adobe Minion Pro; the heading font is Adobe Myriad Condensed; and the code font is Dalton Maag's Ubuntu Mono.

O'REILLY®

Learn from experts.
Become one yourself.

Books | Live online courses
Instant Answers | Virtual events
Videos | Interactive learning

Get started at oreilly.com.

CPSIA information can be obtained
at www.ICGtesting.com
Printed in the USA
JSHW020017050123
35721JS00002B/3